A Minister's Treasury *of* Funeral & Memorial Messages

A Minister's Treasury *of* Funeral & Memorial Messages

Jim Henry

NASHVILLE, TENNESSEE

Copyright © 2003
by Jim Henry
All rights reserved
Printed in the United States of America

0–8054–2575–6

Published by Broadman & Holman Publishers,
Nashville, Tennessee

Dewey Decimal Classification: 252.2
Subject Heading: FUNERAL RITES AND CEREMONIES \ SERMONS

Unless otherwise noted, Scripture quotations are from the Holy Bible, New International Version, copyright © 1973, 1978, 1984 by International Bible Society. Other versions are identified as follows: AMP, The Amplified Bible, Old Testament copyright © 1962, 1964 by Zondervan Publishing House, used by permission, and the New Testament © The Lockman Foundation 1954, 1958, 1987, used by permission. GNB, Good News Bible: The Bible in Today's English Version, © American Bible Society 1966, 1971, 1976; used by permission. KJV, King James Version. Moffatt. The New Testament, a New Translation by James Moffatt. Copyright © 1964 by James The Message, The Message, the New Testament in Contemporary English, © 1993 by Eugene H. Peterson, published by NavPress, Colorado Springs, Colo. Moffatt. Used by permission of Harper & Row, Inc. and Hodder and Stoughton, Ltd. NASB, the New American Standard Bible, © the Lockman Foundation, 1960, 1962, 1963, 1968, 1971, 1972, 1973, 1975, 1977; used by permission. NCV, The Holy Bible, New Century Version, copyright © 1987, 1988, 1991 by Word Publishing, Dallas, Texas 75234. Used by permission. NKJV, New King James Version, copyright © 1979, 1980, 1982, Thomas Nelson, Inc., Publishers.

2 3 4 5 6 7 8 9 10   08 07 06 05 04

Dedication

For the past thirty-five years while serving as pastor of
Two Rivers Baptist Church in Nashville
and First Baptist Church of Orlando,
I have made it my practice to meet with a group of
twelve to twenty men early on Friday mornings.
They have prayed for me, encouraged me, taught me,
loved me, mentored me, held me accountable,
forgiven me, and stood by me.
To these men of God,
some here and some over there with our risen Lord Jesus,
this book is gratefully dedicated.

Contents

Acknowledgments — ix

Part I: Guidelines
1. When the Death Bell Rings — 3

Part II: Memorial Services

Chapter Titles	Type of Service	
2 I'll Hold You Again in Heaven	A Child	15
3 The Life That Conquers	A Student	21
4 She Did What She Could	A Godly Wife, Mother, or Woman	30
5 Finishing Strong	An Elderly Man	38
6 The Secret of the Blessed Man	A Faithful Churchman	46
7 The Faith That Moves God	A Military Person of Faith	54
8 The Sovereign of the Sudden	A Sudden, Unexpected Death	60
9 When Our Why's Cause Us to Wonder	A Tragic Death	67
10 The Windstorms of Life	A Suicide Victim	75

Chapter Titles	Type of Service	
11 Grief: A Season We Must Embrace	One Who Battled a Long Illness	82
12 Coming Late to Jesus	A Recent Convert	88
13 The God of the Second Chance	One Who Returned to the Faith	95
14 Life's Dimensions	Evangelistic	103
15 The Unchangeable Promise of Jesus	Evangelistic	109
16 Looking the Enemy in the Face	General	117
17 Journey to the Father's House	General	122
18 On the Other Side	General	129
19 Assurance for Troubled Days	General	137
20 All the Days of My Life	General	144
21 The Christian's Victory Over Death	General	153
22 The Teacher Called *Death*	General	161
23 What Jesus Did to Death	General	168
24 First Steps	Service for Mothers of Aborted Children	174
Notes		185

Acknowledgments

This book could not have been completed without the tireless work of Sandi Mathis, my executive assistant, who dug through books, files, and papers; translated my scribbles into legible words; and did it without complaint! Marilyn Jeffcoat, who has worked with me on several books, took time from her demanding schedule as educator, speaker, and writer and worked with dedicated effectiveness to proofread, streamline, and give helpful suggestions. My longtime friend and assistant in pastoral care, Jimmy Dusek, contributed the message on "Life's Dimensions." My son-in-law, Stan Campbell, a hospital military chaplain, added the message "The Faith That Moves God" for those who have served in our armed forces. My deepest appreciation goes to our Center for Pregnancy director, Sandy Epperson, for her assistance given on the message concerning a memorial service for an aborted child; to fellow pastor Ike Reighard for suggestions in the message "When Our Why's Cause Us to Wonder"; and the good people of First Baptist Orlando who gave me some extra time off to write as well as prayed for me as I wrote. I acknowledge all these faithful people with heartfelt thanks.

PART I
GUIDELINES

Chapter 1
When the Death Bell Rings

I will never forget the great Baptist preacher Ramsey Pollard relating his first experience officiating a funeral service as a young pastor. He served a country church and was called on to officiate the service of one of its members. The usual apprehensions filled his mind. Seminary had not prepared him for this basic pastoral task.

Somewhere he had read that the officiate was to walk in front of the casket and read Scripture en route to the burial place. Having successfully navigated the service itself, he proceeded out the door in front of the casket to lead the funeral procession to the adjacent cemetery. Opening his Bible, he began to read words of comfort in reverent tones. So engrossed was he in reading that he failed to see the looming cavity of the gravesite and promptly fell foot-first into the six-foot hole!

Panicked by the mortifying thoughts of being in a grave and the obvious embarrassment of his misstep, he scrambled out quickly and began to run. He related that he was grateful a deacon caught him as he was climbing a fence trying to escape. The deacon urged him to return and finish his funeral duties. Pollard said that had he not, he probably would still be running.

Most of us can relate to this story in one way or another. After all, how do you practice doing death services? That's one of the reasons behind my writing this book. With over forty years of walking down the concourse of grief, death, and funeral/memorial services, I have picked up a few things that I believe can be of help to those who are called to assist in one of the most difficult areas of ministry.

The following are practical pointers that have served me well in rural, suburban, and urban settings, while subsequent chapters are written around funeral or memorial messages. Some of the pointers in this chapter are specific while others are more general in nature.

Tip #1: What to Do on Receiving Notification of a Death

1. See the family as soon as possible at the home, hospital, or emergency room.
- Pray with them.
- Listen to them.
- Lend your shoulder.
- Don't use such phrases as, "It must be the will of God," "God needed another angel," etc. They're not ready for that.
- Remember: your presence is what counts.

2. Seek a family member or close family friend with whom you can talk.
- Find someone who is not so emotionally distraught.
- Begin discussing some preliminary planning for the next steps that must be taken.

3. Schedule to go back in the next day or two to plan the memorial service. If possible, see them again before they go to the funeral home.

4. Sometimes you may be asked to assist in the selection of a casket, a burial place, even clothes for the deceased.
- Be helpful when asked, but do not take over.
- Personal note: I try to steer the families away from high-priced accessories that family members often have a tendency to prefer because of their desire to honor their deceased loved ones. Some people have the resources to handle this, but many do not. They can be burdened with debt long into the future, and we can help them by encouraging more moderate costs.

Tip #2: What to Do When Visiting in the Home

1. Ask about the desired place and time for the service: Church, funeral home, or graveside? If they are faithful church members, I encourage the use of the church facilities—a place of warmth, familiarity, memories, and a major part of their lives.

2. Ask about the type of service: memorial if cremation or funeral if body present?

3. Ask who will officiate: pastor, former pastor, staff member, family member, or a friend who is a minister?

4. Ask what type of music is preferred.
- Live, piped-in, tape, or CDs?
- Hymns, praise songs, favorites? Keep in mind the family members who remain, for the loved one is in glory.
- Choir, ensembles, solos, organ, piano, or other music?

5. Ask about favorite Scriptures: family preferences, life passages, or favorite verses of the deceased? Often I have used the deceased's Bible from which to read. This is most appreciated by the family.

6. Ask about any eulogy.
- Pastor can deliver one he has written (if he knows the deceased well), or read one the family has composed.
- Extended family members and friends can also do this.
- Sometimes more than one eulogy is used. If so, be sure to have the participants write the eulogies. This will guard the time as well as help them if they should be overcome with emotion. It also keeps people from rambling.

7. Ask the family if they want a visitation: Night before? Afternoon? Prior to the service? None?

8. Where will the committal be?
- Cremation or ground burial?
- Do they want ashes to be scattered or kept?
- Will there be a military salute, service, or club recognition?

9. Ask about the people they prefer for active pallbearers.
- Family, friends, or both?
- Honorary pallbearers?
- The funeral director will also assist in this.

10. Try to be there with the immediate family as much as possible when planning the service.

Tip #3: What to Do When Scheduling the Service

1. Be sure space is available and the church calendar is checked.

2. Times must be very clear.

3. Contact musicians.

4. If necessary, check with technical assistants for lighting, sound, recording, or videotaping.

5. Prepare the order of service for musicians, tech crew, and funeral directors.

6. Look at a time frame of thirty-five minutes to one hour for most services.

Tip #4: What to Do During the Funeral Home Visit

1. Try to visit with the family during the scheduled funeral home visitation.
- If possible, meet with the family for a few minutes prior to their viewing the body for the first time.
- This is a very emotional time for the family as the reality of death sinks in even more deeply.

- This is especially important if a widow or widower and the deceased does not have extended family or strong church support.

2. At some point, you must address whether the family wants to close the casket before or after the service.

- I usually encourage the family to do so before the service. If the casket is left open during the service—or closed and then reopened—this brings a fresh outpouring of grief, and the worship service's message of encouragement and faith may not come across.
- I encourage the family—as the funeral director probably will—to remove rings, necklaces, jewelry, teddy bears, etc. from the casket. These can be kept in the family and preserved as cherished keepsakes or heirlooms.

3. Seek to give guidance about designating gifts as memorials to the church or a favorite charity or ministry. This provides a living legacy for the deceased.

Tip #5: What to Do During the Service

1. Meet the family in a side room in the church or funeral home for prayer and encouragement. I usually tell them how much their loved one meant to me, outline the procedure for the service, join hands with family members, and pray with them.

2. Precede the family into the service, have the audience rise until the family has been seated, and then ask everyone to be seated.

3. Welcome everyone to the service. Remind them that the purpose of our gathering is to honor Christ and the loved one who has died, as well as to encourage the family.

4. Following this is a good place to read the obituary notes of birthplace and date, names of family members, etc. before proceeding with the planned service.

Tip #6: *What to Do When Concluding the Service*

1. Give clear direction about plans for immediately after dismissal.
- Does the family want one last private time with the body?
- Will there be a reception? If so, where? Some families are now having a private burial, then proceeding to a public memorial service, and afterwards hosting a reception at the church or in their home.
- If going immediately to the cemetery, inform the people of that and of how to form into the processional line.

2. Walk in front of the casket as it is carried out of the church or funeral home. Stand at reverent attention while the casket is placed in the hearse.

3. The funeral director will have your car in the proper place for the procession or will inform you where he wants you to be. This is usually just behind the hearse so that on arrival you can be ready to assist the pallbearers as they take the body to the place of interment.

Tip #7: What to Do at the Graveside

1. Walk before the casket to the appointed place.
2. Stand where the head of the casket is to rest.
3. Wait until everyone is in place before beginning.
4. Speak loudly as being outside absorbs sound quickly.
5. Sometimes the family will desire that a chorus of a familiar hymn or praise song be sung. You or someone else can lead this.
6. Keep the graveside ceremony short. A passage of Scripture on the resurrection and/or the second coming is always appropriate. Pray a brief prayer of committal.
7. If other additions to the graveside ceremony—such as military, lodge, or club—are planned, you may want them to go first.
8. After the closing prayer, shake hands with the immediate family and then step aside.
9. The funeral director will usually conclude the service by directing the pallbearers to place their flowers on the casket.
10. Sometimes, the family wants to stay in place for the covering of the grave. I do not recommend this, but that is a family choice.

I offer these tips for your assistance. Some of the above will vary because of culture, tradition, section of the country, or church practice. But for the most part, they will be appropriate in nearly every situation.

It is my prayer that the following messages will be the seedbed for your inclusions, imagination, and initiative. We all feel as Jane Caudyle, who wrote: "Never does one feel so utterly helpless as trying to speak comfort for great bereavement."[1] Yet, this is our call, our privilege, our responsibility. Only we as ministers of the gospel can be messengers of hope in the midst of grief as we remind our listeners, "It has now been revealed through the appearing of our Savior, Christ Jesus, who has destroyed death and has brought life and immortality to light through the gospel" (2 Tim. 1:10).

PART II

MEMORIAL SERVICES

Chapter 2

I'll Hold You Again in Heaven
(A Child)

2 Samuel 12:15–23

Of all deaths, that of a child is most unnatural and hardest to bear. We expect the old to die. While that kind of separation is always difficult, it comes as no surprise. But the death of a young child or a youth is a different matter. Life with its beauty, wonder, and potential lies ahead for them. Death is a cruel thief when it strikes down the young.

In a way that is different from any other relationship, a child is bone of his parents' bone and flesh of their flesh. When a child dies, part of the parent is buried.[1] So writes Joseph Bayly, who had the sad duty of burying three of his children.

When we lose a child, the effect is widespread. It not only touches the parents, but it can involve siblings, grandparents, friends, and caregivers in a unique way. In the Scripture there is a story that offers us some insight and comfort as we share in this grief. David and Bathsheba's little boy lived only seven days.

I. Reminder That All of Us Can Be Recalled

Life, when it is brief, is a reminder that all of us can be recalled at any time. Life is transitory. "Each man's life is but a breath" (Ps. 39:5). Since we have no guarantee of how long God chooses to grant life, we must maximize the opportunities God gives us. Count every day a blessing. Bless every day by counting.

II. Respond in Grief Until We Find Relief

The illness and death of David's child teaches us how to respond in grief until we find relief. There must be the expression of grief. It must do its work. He did not try to bury his feelings. Grief is a felt response. It must not be smothered. David made a mistake in his grief. He tried to grieve alone. A grief shared is a burden divided. "Rejoice with them that do rejoice, and weep with them that weep" (Rom. 12:15 KJV).

Time will bring some healing, but it will not heal all the wound. Billy Graham wrote, "Time does not heal. It's what you do with the time that heals . . . a long life or a short life are of equal importance to God."[2] If we bury our grief, it is like a toxic waste. It will surface again, and the contamination makes for more trouble. Time alone doesn't overcome sorrow, because sorrow is neutral, a vacuum. Therefore, we turn to the only one who can enable us to deal with our grief: God. "The LORD is close to the brokenhearted and saves those who are crushed in spirit" (Ps. 34:18). Faith in Jesus Christ, who is the resurrection and the life, gives us unexpected strength. We grieve, but not as those who have no hope.

When he was told his child was dead, David made a statement in his grief that has brought comfort to people for generations: "He is dead . . . Can I bring him back again? I will go to him, but he will not return to me" (2 Sam. 12:23). David recognized there was a distinctive line between this world and the next. The child would not come back, but he would go to the child.

How can we be sure that an infant or child has gone to heaven since they may not have accepted Jesus Christ? Because they were too young to have chosen sin, to have reached an accountable age, to have known about sin and salvation through Jesus Christ. The saving work of Christ has reversed sin's curse and covered this little one.

David felt assured of his child's presence in heaven and also that he would be there as well. David had sinned. He was accountable. Why did he have hope? Psalm 51 is the eloquent expression of David's confession of sin and guilt. He sought God's forgiveness, and he received it. The Scriptures are clear: "Whosoever shall call upon the name of the Lord shall be saved" (Rom. 10:13 KJV). This child is in the Lord's presence by God's grace. And through Jesus Christ we will get there, too.

III. Recognize the Sovereignty of God

The death of a child is a time to recognize the sovereignty of God. That growing awareness brings rest to our spirit. God loves children. Scripture clearly illustrates this. Hoping that Jesus might touch them, people brought babies to him. When the disciples saw this, they tried to send them away. But Jesus said to his disciples, "Let these children alone. Don't get between them and me. These children are the kingdom's pride and joy. Mark this: Unless you accept God's kingdom in the simplicity of a child, you'll never get in" (Luke 18:16–17 The Message).

When a child dies, all of us struggle with the purpose and will of God. Every person has a purpose in the divine design. Marshall Shelley and his wife lost a child shortly after birth. In writing about that brief life and their grief, he said, "Why did God create a child to live two minutes? He didn't. He did not create Mandy to live two years. He did not create me to live forty years (or whatever number he may choose to extend my days in this world). God created Toby for eternity. He created each of us for eternity, where we may be surprised to find our true calling, which always seemed just out of reach here on earth."[3]

IV. Release This Child Until We Are Rejoined

Finally, we ask God to give us peace as we seek to release this child until we are rejoined. David said, "Can I bring him back again? I will go to him, but he will not return to me" (2 Sam. 12:23). David's response and insight carries penetrating truth for us. The Scriptures tell us that he went to the house of the Lord and worshiped, comforted his wife, and returned to the business of life (vv. 20, 24, 29).

This child has brought joy and taught us so much about the precious gift of a child. Though grief hammers at our hearts and

I'll Hold You Again in Heaven

the memories will always be cherished, we realize, because of Jesus and his victory over death, that there will be a reunion.

Kenneth McFarland told of an item he found on the obituary page of the newspaper in a small southern town. It read, "Billy, it was just a year ago today that you left us and the sunshine went out of our lives. But, we turned on the headlights and we're going on . . . and Billy, we shall keep on doing the best we can until that glorious day when we shall see you again." It was signed simply "Love, the family." No names, just a simple testimony to the kind of faith that enables a person to go on in the face of sorrow and death.[4]

Until we come to that day when all mysteries, purposes, and plans of God are sorted out for us in the day when we shall see God face-to-face, let us be thankful that this life has enriched us and made us the better because of it.

Nathaniel Timothy Kuck was a beautiful child, who spent most of his four and one-half years overcoming physical obstacles. When he went to be with the Lord, a neighbor, blessed by his life and the comments of his father at the memorial service, wrote these words as if the father, Tim, were writing:

As I look back on what the years did bring,
I wouldn't change a single thing.
He taught me how to appreciate life,
He taught my girls, and taught my wife.
Now he dances with David and fishes with Peter;
I can't imagine a life that's neater.

When I look back, the conclusion I draw
'Twas me who got the longest straw.[5]

This child belongs to God. Today we release his hands as God has grasped them over there, and he will never let them go. "The key to your child's casket is not in the hands of the keeper of the cemetery. But the key is in the hands of the Son of God, and he will come some morning and use it."[6] "'I am the Alpha and the Omega,' says the Lord God, 'who is, and who was, and who is to come, the Almighty'" (Rev. 1:8).

Chapter 3

The Life That Conquers
(A Student)

Romans 8:35–39

[The memorial service for a student is a time of deep sorrow and reflection. Young people sometimes feel immune to death and tragedy. When it strikes, they are hard hit. Emotions run high. Memories of regret and happiness comingle. In such a time, the pastor has a golden opportunity to bring comfort, hope, and the message of salvation.

In planning with the family for a memorial service, the following suggestions serve as helpful guidelines for a meaningful tribute to their deceased student. These include: music by the school choirs, an opening and closing prayer by a classmate, and remembering the student with brief testimonials by friends, classmates, or a student pastor. The testimonials should include some humorous memories, as well as those of high moments of accomplishment or service to the Lord, church, school, friends, and community. A video always carries images that bring out the best of the student's life. Worship music should be that which speaks to eternal truths, as well as to the contemporary ear of their classmates.]

Every death reminds us that our time on earth is limited. We are never guaranteed a tomorrow. We only have today. That is a reminder to all of us to live life to the fullest, to love life, to appreciate life, and to make life count. Jesus, who lived only thirty-three years, reminds us that he came that we might have life and have it to the full.

What is a full life? What is real life? What makes a life—though short in number of years—a life that conquers? Paul, one of the most brilliant men who ever lived and a devoted follower of Jesus Christ, understood that kind of life. Near the end of his own life, he wrote, "We are more than conquerors through him who loved us" (Rom. 8:37).

Webster's dictionary uses several synonyms for the word *conquer*. It means "to vanquish, subdue, reduce, overcome, overthrow." These conquerors are what a football coach calls "impact players." Impact players influence our lives. They are people who make a difference wherever they are, whatever their age. These individuals hold certain things in common.

I. Makes the Right Choice

The first thing they hold in common is that they make the right choice. Years ago, Joshua, a great soldier for God, spoke these words: "Choose for yourselves this day whom you will serve . . . as for me and my household, we will serve the LORD" (Josh. 24:15).

A young man approached Jesus and asked him, "What must I do to inherit eternal life?" Jesus' response was, "Follow me" (Mark 10:17, 21). We are very valuable to God. So valuable that he gave his Son Jesus Christ to die in our place and granted us the privilege to choose to live with him forever. We must make that choice.

Adam Burtle, a student atheist from Woodinville, Washington, startled many eBay searchers when he ran this item: "20-year-old Seattle boy's SOUL, hardly used. Please realize, I make no warranties as to the condition of the soul. As of now, it is near mint condition with only minor scratches." The bidding had reached four hundred dollars when eBay officials removed the listing and suspended Burtle from the site.[1]

How much is our soul worth? "This is how we know what love is: Jesus Christ laid down his life for us" (1 John 3:16). The life that conquers realizes that we are very special to God, and that we have made a personal decision to choose him to be our Savior and Lord. This is the most important choice you will ever make.

II. Fulfills God's Purpose

The second thing that conquerors in Christ hold in common is a life that fulfills God's purpose. God has a purpose and plan for every one of us. "Before I formed you in the womb I knew you, before you were born I set you apart" (Jer. 1:5). Every person should ask himself the questions that a teacher once asked a group of students to ponder: *What do you live for? How do you get it? Is it worth it?*

Dr. Seuss, whose writings have entertained children for years, spoke at a commencement at Lake Forest College, outside Chicago. He decided to make it the world's shortest address and get it down to one minute, fourteen seconds.

Dr. Seuss talked about an uncle who placed an order for popovers at a restaurant. As he gazed at the roll of pastry lying before him, he concluded it was mostly air. He made the philosophical observation that in life a person would be very wise to do a lot of "spitting out the hot air" that passes for wisdom in a dumbed-down world.

God's purpose for your life includes the big things and the little things. He has a plan for your education, your school activities, your involvement in his church, whom you are to marry, and what you do for a living.

Many students feel like the student who was asked by Lloyd Ogilvie, chaplain of the U.S. Senate, "What is your greatest need and your greatest fear?" To which he responded, "Sir, my greatest need is to know God's perfect will for my life. My greatest fear is that I will miss it, or if I know it, that I will resist doing it."[2]

You can be sure of knowing God's purpose for your life through a genuine relationship with him. He is your Father, and he is the one who will communicate with you. He will communicate that purpose through his Word—the Scriptures, godly counselors, and circumstances. He will lead you as you release your will to him.

That release can be best pictured by imagining a blank piece of paper. Sign your name at the bottom, and then let God fill in the blanks. You will be in for the ride of your life, whatever its length may be.

Someone has said:
To know Him is to love Him;
to love Him is to trust Him;
to trust Him is to obey Him;
to obey Him is to be blessed.[3]

In the National Gallery of Art hang some of the great original masterpieces—done by the artists themselves in their own oils with their own strokes. They are masterpieces. In a little shop at the gallery you can purchase copies of the originals for a dollar. Someone has pointed out that each one of us must decide whether we will "give ourselves to Jesus Christ and become the divine original God intended or whether we will refuse Christ . . . and remain a cheap copy of what we might have been."[4] The life that conquers is a life that is intentional in knowing and doing God's will.

III. Conquers with Courage

The third characteristic of a life that conquers is a life of courage. God has never promised us an easy life, but he has assured us that he will give us courage to face the difficulties, struggles, heartaches, and disappointments of life. At least sixteen times in the Bible, God encourages us to take courage. We need courage to fight prejudice, to speak up for those no one will speak up for, to keep our lives pure, to be a friend to those whom others may leave out, to face fears, to try again when we have failed, to live our convictions that come from character formed by eternal truths, and to persevere.

The movie *Braveheart* tells the story of William Wallace, probably the greatest hero of Scotland. His life and legend have been strong in Scotland for nearly seven hundred years. William Wallace was a committed Christian. When England tried to claim Scotland, Wallace would not surrender to the king of England. He fought and defeated the English in several key battles. The king tried to gain his cooperation by offering him position, titles, money, and land. Wallace refused.

His courage was so contagious that it rubbed off on Robert the Brave, the logical successor to become the next king of Scotland. Robert's father was a coward who was secretly cooperating with the king of England. He persuaded his son to do the same. Disguised as a masked knight, the son was dispatched to kill Wallace. In combat, Wallace got the upper hand, unmasked Robert the Brave, and was shocked to see his betrayal. Rather than killing him, Wallace rode away to safety.

Young Robert realized he was a Judas, a betrayer. He returned to his father in anguish and confessed that his actions were tearing him apart. His father said, "All men betray. All lose heart." The son replied, "I don't want to lose heart. I want to believe as he [Wallace] does. I will never be on the wrong side again."

Someone has observed that there are not many bravehearts left. "There are many faint of heart. The bravehearts have always been in the minority."[5] The life that conquers is a life of courage.

IV. Marks Life with Service

The life that conquers is a life that is marked by service. Through the centuries, God has used youth to serve him and mankind. One of Jesus' disciples, John, was probably a teenager when he began to follow Jesus. Mary, the mother of Jesus, was a young woman in her teens when she was chosen to bring God's Son into the world.

Sometimes you may feel like Charlie Brown in the *Peanuts* comic strip. Charlie and his little girlfriend were looking up at the millions of stars above. Charlie said, "Space is too large." In the next frame, Lucy said, "We don't really need all that room . . . most of those planets and stars are way too big!" She continued in the next frame, "The whole solar system needs readjusting." Charlie turned to her and said, "What can we, as individuals, do?"[6]

You can be different from the crowd around you. You can take God seriously and make a profound difference wherever he places you. Peter stated this plainly: "Each one should use whatever gift he has received to serve others" (1 Pet. 4:10).

In Orlando, Florida, the young athlete, popular student, and active Christian Brent Bolin was killed in an automobile accident. His sudden death grieved his family and all who knew him. Months later, the weight room at his school was dedicated in his honor. Brent's mother read these words, which speak so eloquently of dedicating what God has given you to him: "You are God's opportunity in your day. He has waited ages for a person just like you. Go where he sends you to go. Do what he gives you to do. Do you know him? Now, go and make him known by living a noble life. Do "godly-good" for those around you.

- "If he has blessed you with spiritual strength, be noble by praying for those who are weak in their faith. Remind them that they, too, are Jesus' own.
- "If he has blessed you with physical strength, be noble by defending those who struggle each day with those who seek to harm them. Speak up and speak out against hatred, prejudice, and malice.
- "If he has blessed you with mental strength and intellectual abilities, be noble by discovering a cure for a disease, tell the gospel in a language never spoken, and find solutions to elevate your brothers and sisters out of misery.
- "If he has blessed you to be socially strong and if making friends comes easily to you, be noble by befriending those who feel that they don't belong and struggle to be accepted . . . help free them from their loneliness.
- "If he has blessed you with emotional strength and you are content with who you are, be noble by 'standing on the wall' and encourage those who are saddened by life by building them up in Christ. You will strengthen them and help them find joy.
- "If he has blessed YOU with artistic strength in all its diversity, be noble by using these talents to show the world the divine, unlimited beauty of God.

"Do not refuse God his opportunity that he seeks through you. Remember, there is only one like you on this earth *and there is no other*.

"In Hebrews 12, the author says to us, 'Run the race that is before us . . . never give up . . . never quit. Keep your eyes on Jesus who began and finished the race of life. He finished strong, so we too can finish strong' (Heb. 12:1–3 The Message)."[7]

Paul's words were autobiographical. Out of his own personal tribulations, he challenges us to "be more than conquerors." Literally, he says, "We are super conquerors!" Not just victors, but "super victors"![8] Today we may go away with our grief, but we do not go away defeated. Because Jesus Christ conquered sin, death, and all evil powers, so do we when we choose him as Savior, fulfill his purpose in our lives, live a life of courage, and serve him and our fellow man nobly. We win! We are eternal impact players! We are super conquerors!

Chapter 4

She Did What She Could
(A Godly Wife, Mother, or Woman)

Mark 14:3–9

We are here to focus not so much on what we have lost, but on what we have gained because this godly woman came into our lives. We are here because we have hope: not hope with a question mark, but hope with an exclamation point! We are here to acknowledge that death is an enemy, not a friend. It is an enemy of God and of us—an enemy because it destroys life that is in contrast to God, the creator and author of life. We are here to praise Jesus Christ, the conqueror of our ancient enemy. Our hearts and minds are riveted on the only one who has said, "I am the resurrection and the life. He who believes in me will live, even though he dies" (John 11:25).

Shortly before Jesus was crucified, he came to the home of Simon the leper. They were having a celebration because of his miraculous healing. Among the guests were some cherished friends of Jesus: Martha, Lazarus, and Mary. While they were talking and enjoying the event, an astounding thing took place. Mary, who loved to sit at the feet of Jesus, knelt unexpectedly beside him, shattered the neck of a flask of expensive perfume, and poured it on Jesus' head and feet. She wiped the rapidly evaporating perfume from his feet and dried them with her hair. It was a spellbinding moment. This act of devotion is one of the most incredible stories of devotion in Scripture. It speaks of the love, humility, and sacrifice in Mary's heart. In this magnificent moment, we see the heart of a woman who did all she could for her Savior, as did this one whose life we celebrate today. Her actions were symbolic of her life—a life broken and poured out for Christ and others.

I. Prolific Act

See it as a prolific act. The alabaster vial probably contained perfume imported from India. It was worth a year's income of a day laborer. A day laborer earned about twenty cents a day, which is equivalent to about sixty dollars for a year's work. With the inflation of today, we are looking at the equivalent of a gift worth thousands of dollars. To some it was a waste. To Mary, it was the expression of an extravagant love. In this act we see the splendor of a giving, generous heart.

When someone has done something important and good for us, we must express gratitude. At the height of William Faulkner's writing career, it was reported that his income was so great that it amounted to ten dollars a word. One enterprising young man wrote to Faulkner, saying, "Enclosed is ten dollars. Please send me one of your best words." In reply, William Faulkner sent back this word: "Thanks."[1]

The lady we remember today was also a generous and thoughtful woman.

II. Providential Act

Mary's act was also a providential act. Jesus reminded the bewildered audience, "You will not always have me" (Mark 14:7). Some opportunities come to us only one time. We must act at the prompting to do the right thing at the right time. It has been said that opportunity does not send letters of introduction.[2]

Priceless moments remind us of the value of time. The samurai would begin his day meditating on his own death. He would even visualize all the ways he could die on that very day.[3] The Bible constantly reminds us of the brevity and uncertainty of life. "You do not even know what will happen tomorrow. What is your life? You are a mist that appears for a little while and then vanishes" (James 4:14).

III. Practical Act

Mary did all she could. We readily see it as a practical act (Mark 14:8). For her, there was no time to go to the market, to prepare a meal, or to weave a robe. Leave that to Martha or others. Some people are theoretical and some are practical. She did the thing nearest and dearest with what she had. Love does what it needs to do with whatever is available. "Love is not really blind. It has the most generous of eyes. Professor Henry Drummond used to say if you buy a box, it must be flawless. But if your little son, with his rough tools, makes you a box, very probably it has a hundred faults. Yet you appreciate that clumsy workmanship far more than what you purchased in the market, because it's the work of the little boy you love."[4] How powerful is the action of love that does the right thing at the right time with the insight of practicality.

IV. Perceptive Action

Mary's ministry was also a perceptive action (Mark 14:8b). Jesus had often spoken of his death. He mentioned at least seventeen times that he would die and be resurrected. But his followers didn't get the picture. Sometimes the truth nearest us is the truth that evades us. Their spiritual ears didn't hear, but Mary's did.

Mary knew that a person who died as a criminal—according to the law of that day—was denied the customary anointing oils and perfumes. At Jesus' birth, the wise men brought gifts that included the gift of myrrh. Myrrh was used by the Egyptians for embalming and by the Hebrews ceremonially. In the Old and New Testaments, we see it used as a symbol of blessing and life. Mary's action highlighted not only her devoted love, but her spiritually perceptive spirit. Jesus would die, but not unsaluted! The conduct of our lives is a strong indicator of the presence of Christ that enables us to say and do those things that reflect his heart.

We must be grateful for those thoughtful people whom God's grace places in our journey of life. They know when to say the right words, when we need encouragement, how to send a card or E-mail when our burdens are heavy, how to share a gift when the bank account is low. They stop to pray when we do not know the way, or they put an arm around us when a touch rejuvenates our spirit. Have you ever been on the receiving end of such a perceptive and thoughtful act? These acts are in the category of what one might call "those things we are willing to count, anxious to multiply, and reluctant to divide."[5]

V. Perpetual Transaction

Mary's gift has been forever memorialized. It was a gesture that took one brief moment, but it became a perpetual transaction. Jesus promised it would never be forgotten: "I tell you the truth, wherever the gospel is preached throughout the world, what she has done will also be told, in memory of her" (Mark 14:9 The Message). As we celebrate and remember the life of this godly woman, we are fulfilling what Jesus said of Mary over two thousand years ago.

When we do what we can, it has a long-term effect in the spiritual world that continues to touch lives for many years. At Christmas time in a rural church, the congregation privately collected money to give the young pastor and his growing family a cash gift for Christmas. When the gift had been gratefully received, and most of the people had left the sanctuary, an elderly woman—who lived on a fixed income—pulled the pastor aside and timidly put a five-dollar-bill in his hand. He tried to refuse, but she insisted, telling him that the Lord told her to do it, and he must not rob her of the joy of giving. In later years of ministry, he said that this one small act was the planting of a seed that taught him to become a gracious giver.

It's been said that Jesus has a lot of strange things in his treasury: widows' pennies, cups of water, broken alabaster vases, ruined recipe boxes. Has he anything of yours? Do you feel the impulse to do something beautiful for God? Then crown it with action.[6]

Our beloved did what she could. No better words can be spoken of any person than these. That kind of loving devotion characterized the life of the one we remember today. This kind of woman is a gift to her husband, children, family, church, neighborhood, and above all, her Lord. Perhaps this is best captured in these words: "For God loved the world so much that he gave his only Son, so that everyone who believes in him may not die but have eternal life" (John 3:16 GNB).

We have all played the mental game of "What If." What if I rubbed a magic lamp and a genie gave me three wishes? What if a good fairy appeared and gave me a magic charm with great powers? We may not have any basis to believe in genies or fairies. But what if God himself appeared to us and said, "Hold out your hands. I want to give you a most wonderful gift. This gift has great power: both to help and, if misused, to harm. The power of the gift will grow as you become familiar with it. As you develop the ability to draw power from the gift, you will find great satisfaction and fulfillment from the things you are able to accomplish through it . . . things that will affect generations to come and will have an eternal effect on many lives. In preparing this gift for you, I have taken into consideration your capabilities and desires. You will find the powers of this gift will both compliment and supplement your own. You will find the capacity to accomplish tasks you would not have undertaken before, and where you have strengths now you will greatly surpass your old ideals. Before you accept it, let me tell you there are responsibilities that go along with the gift."

Would you interrupt at this point and say, "Sure, God. Just toss it in the back of the car and I'll check it out at my earliest convenience." I think not. You would not take lightly a gift offered by God.

God continues, "You must not mistreat this gift for although it is very durable, it is also very fragile. It can be damaged and great harm can come to you and many other people if this is allowed. You will be called on by many to share the powers of this gift, because others will need it also. But you must use discretion and protect the gift from misuse. I will be with you, will strengthen and guide you. But if you think these conditions will be too difficult, you must not accept the gift. The gift that I have prepared for you is your mate. It is my plan that this be a mutual gift. For you see, I have also prepared you in a similar way as a gift.

Although you will not completely understand this, the gift, though it is for a lifetime, might better be considered a loan."

I have come to understand in the years since I first had these thoughts that the gift was not the person of my mate. For God maintained ownership as she really belonged to him. But the gift was time we would have together to enjoy each other and the work that God would give us.[7]

This devoted follower of Jesus Christ would urge you to give your best to him. If you are a Christian, renew your pledge to do what you can. If you have never received Jesus Christ as God's best for you as your personal Savior and Lord, there is no better time than now. Jesus is truly the best that God can do. God's alabaster perfume was wrapped in a human body. His was a body that was broken for our sins. This became the greatest gift of all. That truth is captured in these familiar words: "This is how we know what love is: Jesus Christ laid down his life for us" (1 John 3:16 GNB).

At the end of his life, Michelangelo expressed it this way: "I have loved my friends and family. I have loved God and all His creation. I have loved life and now I love death as its natural termination . . . knowing that although Christendom may be over—Christ lives!"[8]

Chapter 5

Finishing Strong (Hanging Up the Spikes)
(An Elderly Man)

2 Timothy 4:6–8

One of baseball's greatest players was Lou Gehrig. Known as the "Iron Man" for playing more games consecutively than any other player except Cal Ripkin, Gehrig was stricken with an incurable disease, a painful shrinking of body tissue for which there is no cure, a condition later named Gehrig's Disease. After fighting this health battle, he was forced to tearfully say farewell to his colleagues and friends at Yankee Stadium. Gehrig had to hang up the spikes.

That's a reality for all of us at some point in our lives. Paul had reached that milestone in his life when he wrote to his successor, the young pastor Timothy. In fifty-two words this nearly seventy-year-old man penned his testimony and challenge. Writing from a dungeon, Paul's words are timeless reminders of the power of a life that is lived well and finishes strong. [*Read 2 Tim. 4:6–8 at this point.*]

I. Confident

Because of his relationship to Jesus Christ, a person who finishes strong is confident in the face of death. Paul used the term *departure* as a picture of death (v. 6). It is a word that in maritime usage means "to weigh anchor by the loosening of the ropes." It is also an army term meaning "to break down the tent and leave camp." Paul saw himself as a man on a journey heading for the next stop. In his other writings, Paul described death as "at home with the Lord" in 2 Corinthians 5:8; "gain" and "with Christ" in Philippians 1:21, 23; and "fallen asleep in him [Christ]" in 1 Thessalonians 4:14.

J. Redford Wilson, who entered the hospital for what would be the last time, was told by the doctors that his chances of survival were small. "But," they said, "surgery might help."

Even so, the surgery itself contained risk and his chances were marginal. With steady eye-to-eye contact and a twinkling smile, Redford unshakably replied, "Either way, Doc, I win."[1]

Death is a reality that must be looked squarely in the eye. Martin Luther said, "Even in the best of health we should always have death before our eyes. We will not expect to remain on this earth forever, but will have one foot in the air, so to speak."[2]

Only Jesus Christ has the key to victory over death. He conquered death when he rose from its cold clutches two thousand years ago. Because Jesus Christ lives, he offers to everyone the opportunity to overcome death.

In the mid-nineteenth century, a young lawyer named Abraham Lincoln went to observe what transpired at a slave auction. He saw black Americans being chained like cattle and auctioned off to the highest bidder. Eventually, a young woman was brought to the block, and bidding started. Lincoln put in a bid, which was countered by another. He bid higher and was countered again. Finally, he outbid all the others and the auctioneer proclaimed, "Sold!"

Then the slave traders brought the young woman off the block and set her at Lincoln's feet. He reached down, unlocked the chains, and said, "You're free."

The emancipated slave looked at Lincoln with a quizzical look and asked, "What does it mean to be free?"

Lincoln responded, "It means that you can think anything you want to think, you can say anything you want to say, you can go wherever you want."

The reality of her newfound freedom began to sink in and, with tears streaming down her cheeks, she said, "Then I will go with you."

That's what Jesus wants to do with us. He came to find us, to forgive us, and to free us from the power of sin.[3] Finishing strong can only be done by a life that has chosen Christ as Savior and Lord.

II. Concentrated

To finish strong is to have a concentrated life. A concentrated life to the lordship of Jesus Christ results in a focused, centered life. Paul looks in the rearview mirror in verse 7: "I have fought the good fight." The word *fight* comes from a word from which we derive our word *agency*. It's the picture of an athlete in any contact sport leaving it all on the field—giving everything he has. It is to give a total effort.

Paul found many adversaries in his life: sin, guilt, spiritual oppression from demonic forces, violent opponents, physical problems, internal fears. Yet, Paul never failed to give his all. The time to do that is now. One of the greatest saboteurs of dreams and goals is that little word, *someday*.

Zig Ziglar tells the story of the man who went next door to borrow his neighbor's lawnmower. The neighbor explained that he couldn't let him use the mower because all the flights had been cancelled from New York to Los Angeles. The borrower asked him what cancelled flights had to do with him borrowing his lawnmower. "It doesn't have anything to do with it," the neighbor replied. "But if I don't want to let you use my lawnmower, one excuse is as good as another."

The same is true for any person looking to put off the work that brings him closer to reaching his goals. "Someday when I have the time or money." "Someday I'll study up on that." "Someday after the kids have moved out." "Someday . . ."[4] To finish strong is to give your best now.

Paul also had concentrated on completing his work. "I have finished the race" (v. 7). Paul always kept his objectives in front of him. "I consider my life worth nothing to me, if only I may finish the race and complete the task the Lord Jesus has given me—the task of testifying to the gospel of God's grace" (Acts 20:24).

Many people start well but do not finish well. A prominent pastor listed the names of twenty-four young men who were ministering with him in their twenties. Thirty years later, only three of those twenty-four were still in the ministry.

Life is most fulfilling when it is filled with purposes. Purpose becomes the driving force of contentment. George Bernard Shaw expressed it this way: "I want to be thoroughly used up when I die, for the harder I work, the more I live . . . life is no brief candle to me. It is a sort of splendid torch, which I've got a hold of for a moment, and I want to make it burn as brightly as possible before handing it on to future generations."[5]

Finishing strong also means to play by the rules. Paul said, "I have kept the faith" (v. 7). Athletes in the Greek Olympic games took an oath to compete with honesty and integrity. There are several possible meanings to this term, "keep the faith." Among those meanings is "keeping faithful to one's commitment to Christ." The person who finishes strong is the person who keeps the faith.

Modern culture knows little of this kind of life. However, it is a commodity that builds strong marriages, communities, churches, and nations. How does that kind of life become a reality?

Steve Farrar, in his book *Finishing Strong*, suggests that it's done by four steps:

1. Stay in the Scriptures. "Do not let this Book of the Law depart from your mouth; meditate on it day and night, so that you may be careful to do everything written in it" (Josh. 1:8).
2. Stay close to a friend. "Encourage one another daily, as long as it is called Today, so that none of you may be hardened by sin's deceitfulness" (Heb. 3:13).
3. Stay away from other women. "Do not let your heart turn to her ways or stray into her paths. Many are the victims she has brought down . . . Her house is a highway to the grave" (Prov. 7:25–27).
4. Stay alert to the tactics of the enemy. "Be self-controlled and alert. Your enemy the devil prowls around . . . looking for someone to devour. Resist him, standing firm in the faith" (1 Pet. 5:8–9).

A life that finishes strong resonates with the words of Josiah Gilbert Holland:

> God, give us men, a time like this demands
> Strong minds, great hearts, true faith and ready
>   hands;
> Men whom the lust of fire does not kill,
> Men whom the spoils of fire cannot buy,
> Men who possess opinions and a will,
> Men who have honor, men who will not lie.[6]

III. Contemplates

The strong finisher is the man who contemplates the future. "Now there is in store for me the crown of righteousness, which the Lord, the righteous Judge, will award to me on that day—and not only to me, but also to all who have longed for his appearing" (v. 8). The crown about which Paul writes was made up of laurel leaves formed into a wreath and presented to the victor in athletic events. Paul affirms that on "that day," the day of the Lord's return and at the judgment seat of Christ, he will receive this award. It is a reward the Lord will present not only to Paul, but to "all who have longed for his appearing."

Someone has said, "Finishing is a rare and valuable commodity. Completing the task. Staying till the final whistle. Driving the last nail. Never walking away. No pulling back. No drifting. No waffling . . . finishes have certain qualities."[7]

The world is looking for men and women who finish strong. Today as we admire and pay our respects to this man of faith, it's a good time to examine our journey of life. Is there any change in lifestyle or attitude we need to make? Is there anything not settled with Jesus Christ or someone else that needs to be settled? How would we recap our lives? Could we say what Paul said in this powerful farewell?

When Sir Walter Raleigh laid his new coat on the ground so that Queen Elizabeth might walk without getting her shoes dirty, he knew that there is no price too great for royalty. Whatever he could do to honor the queen of England should be done. And whatever we can do to honor the King of kings should be done now.[8] We can be like the writer to the Hebrews who wrote these words: "Since we are surrounded by so great a cloud of witnesses, let us lay aside every weight, and the sin which so easily ensnares us, and let us run with endurance the race that is set before us, looking unto Jesus, the author and finisher of our faith" (Heb. 12:1–2 NKJV). We should make it the priority of our lives to finish strong. And in some measure to be able to say to our Lord Jesus Christ, who taught us how to finish well: "I have glorified thee on the earth: I have finished the work which thou gavest me to do" (John 17:4 KJV).

To finish strong does not mean living a perfect life. Every man has his successes and failures. Guilt and regret must not dog the rest of your life. Solomon wrote, "For though a righteous man falls seven times, he rises again, but the wicked are brought down by calamity" (Prov. 24:16). You can finish strong. Determine today to run the best you can.

Chapter 6

The Secret of the Blessed Man
(A Faithful Churchman)

Psalm 1:1–6

Every dad has his favorite chair, the place where he drops at the end of a tough day to watch the news, to read, to catch an athletic event, and sometimes to sleep in. It's the familiar place. You've seen him there many times.

Every husband and every father also sits in some other chairs. John Maxwell had names for these metaphorical chairs:

- The Chair of Compromise: the chair of "lukewarmness" toward God, connecting with God only when it's convenient.
- The Chair of Conflict: the chair marked by coldness toward God because of no relationship to him. Since this man doesn't personally know God, he lives in conflict—pushed and pulled by everything the world has to offer.
- The Chair of Commitment: those men who occupy this chair live for God and seek him with all their heart.[1]

The Bible describes such a man. He is found in Psalm 1. [*Read this psalm at this point.*] The man whose life is being celebrated today is the kind of life we see in this psalm.

1. Character

Note first the character of the man who is blessed. The word *blessed* means "happy" in the Beatitudes. The man who is blessed is the man who makes it his purpose to be a godly man. How does a man become a godly man and mature into the nature of his Savior? It begins with three refusals, three choices he makes.

First, he "does not walk in the counsel of the wicked" (v. 1). *Wicked people* are godless people. They live their lives horizontally. They have no vertical dependence on the God of heaven, the supernatural. They do it their way. Their lives are marked by independence. The blessed man does not expose himself to their lifestyles or philosophies.

Second, the blessed man does not "stand in the way of sinners" (v. 1). He is careful where he hangs out and spends time. He is spiritually discerning. He is alert to moral distinctives. *Sinners* are people who miss the mark. Their goals and values are counter to the ways of God. Their god is self.

Third, the blessed man does not "sit in the seat of mockers" (v. 1). Mockers are cynical and skeptical. Life is lived for their own purposes. Their ambitions and goals are built on the idea of the superhero—the macho man—who pulls himself up by his own bootstraps and does not need the assistance of God or man. The blessed man is the opposite of the ungodly. The ungodly begin to walk, then stand, then sit, and become comfortable with their lives apart from God—a steady progression downward. But the blessed man has his heart set on piety, purity, and purpose—all in the context of a heart set as the psalmist states at another place: "Delight yourself in the LORD and he will give you the desires of your heart. Commit your way to the LORD; trust in him and he will do this" (Ps. 37:4–5).

II. Conduct

The blessed man's secret begins in character formed by his relationship to Jesus Christ. It shows itself in the conduct of his life. The ability to conduct life at the highest level doesn't just happen. It is the derivative of a man who is pursuing the heart of God. How does a man get to have the character of God so that he conducts his life in such a way that it mirrors his Creator and Lord? Verse 2 gives us this open secret: "His delight is in the law of the LORD."

What is God's law? It is his requirements for man. They are summed up in Jesus' words: "'Love the Lord your God with all your heart and with all your soul and with all your mind.' This is the first and greatest commandment. And the second is like it: 'Love your neighbor as yourself'" (Matt. 22:37–39). God's law gives us the precepts of life. They are God's boundary lines. They are guiding principles which a man sees as his north star, the compass of life.

III. Conclusion

The blessed man's life has a happy conclusion (v. 3). His is a tree planted "by streams of water." The man who is in Christ is, as Christ promised, "a spring of water welling up to eternal life" (John 4:14). That tree does two things. First, it "yields its fruit in season" (v. 3). Jesus said, "If a man remains in me and I in him, he will bear much fruit" (John 15:5). Second, his "leaf does not wither" (v. 3). He will be an ever-bearing evergreen!

Unashamed. Examine some of the fruit of the tree of this blessed man. It can be seen in his unashamed personal faith and commitment to Jesus Christ. Jesus said, "Whoever acknowledges me before men, I will also acknowledge him before my Father in heaven. But whoever disowns me before men, I will disown him before my Father in heaven" (Matt. 10:32–33).

Unmistakable commitment. He was unmistakably committed to the church of our Lord Jesus. He took joy in counting himself a member of the church. He understood that "Christ loved the church and gave himself up for her" (Eph. 5:25), and that "to him be glory in the church and in Christ Jesus" (Eph. 3:21). In a day of noncommittal, anonymous Christianity, he understood the critical importance of the community of faith.

Untiring service. In the church, he not only was a faithful member, but he was untiring in his service to Christ through the church. He did more than occupy a pew. He understood that ministry was not an option, but a joyful responsibility to pour out his life helping others to know Christ, to follow him, and to be a servant in time of need. He imitated his Lord, who took upon himself the form of a servant and taught us, "The greatest among you will be your servant" (Matt. 23:11).

Unconditional love. His life was marked by an unconditional love for his family. He kept his marriage vows to his wife, being faithful unto death. He made a promise to God and her, didn't look for an excuse to get out of it, and did not go back on it. He remembered the words of our Lord Jesus: "'And the two will become one flesh.' So they are no longer two, but one. Therefore, what God has joined together, let man not separate" (Mark 10:8–9). It has been said that most women do not want their men to die for them. They want their man to live for them.[2] He lived his life joyfully with his sweetheart of the years.

That love was seen in his pride for his family. He was a role model for his children. He understood the importance of being a father. *Newsweek* published an article on fathering in which a dad told a reporter that when he takes care of his children on the weekend his friends sometimes say, "Oh, you're babysitting." "No, I'm not," he replies. "I'm being their father."[3]

He did not pretend to be flawless; however, his lack of perfection did not keep him from striving to be his best.

One woman, reflecting on her father's role in her life, wrote him a letter on Father's Day and stated well her view of her dad. This is reflective of this dad.

And who are you!

The author of my memories and dreams

The Secret of the Blessed Man

My teachers, prophets, and preachers
Sculptor of my soul . . .
Stepping back now—ever receding
Pushing me forward, upward,
Yet always there when I call.

Fathers,
Pied pipers playing horns of plenty—
Understanding, caring, concerned,
Aging, yet never growing old
Reaching out, but not holding back,
Love incarnate—

Ever striving to understand my world
Bending, but never breaking
Praying I'll find that rainbow's end
Wishing the path were better marked
And knowing that Never-Never Land
Will one day change into Tomorrowland.

Wanting to ease the pain—
Seeing in the future, the past
Glimpsing in the teacher, the mother,
the grandchild, the meaning of life—
Asking the other Father to take my hand
When you let go
And to guide my star.
What I am and will be

Is because you are.
Thank you."[4]

Charlie Shedd, author of many family books and the syndicated newspaper column, *Strictly for Dads*, once told about listening to a famous child psychiatrist read a paper on "theological duplications in the father-child relationship." His article began by saying that he himself was a believer. And then he made this announcement: "No little child will think more of God than he thinks of his own father!"[5] This man's family did not have to run after phony gods or models. They found a father who had a deep love for them and sought to point them to the perfect Father.

IV. Contrast

The contrast of this real kind of man and the world's kind of man is seen in verses 4 and 5. "You're not at all like the wicked, who are mere windblown dust—without defense in court, unfit company for innocent people. GOD charts the road you take, the road they take is Skid Row" (Ps. 1:4–6 The Message). The road this father and dad has taken is the high road. The road of a blessed man. The road that has taken him to the end of life's journey to join his eternal Father.

In his dying, he clung to Jesus Christ. His passing can do for you and for others what the passing of his dad did for Walter Wangerin Jr. As his dad lay dying, "Walter Junior" wrote:

> For forty-three years, consciously or not—it
> doesn't matter—my father has been preparing me for

this crisis; and it is right to plead with every Christian parent: Please, never make a secret of your faith. For the sake of your children against the day when you will surely die; in order to transfigure, then, their grief into something more healing than destroying, assure them with cheerful conviction, even in the good, green days of childhood, that you live and you shall die in the arms of Jesus, in whose love is life and everlasting life. Let them know that you know. Your knowledge shall be their precious gift. Their freedom. I believe his believing. If his dying doesn't destroy him, it doesn't destroy me either. If it is for him a beginning, it can be for me a passage—hope has a marvelous staying power—and this is the evidence of our common, hopeful, liberating faith, that I am writing to you now, my father, my senior, this letter fully as formal as the letter you sent to us, fully as honest and unafraid as yours. On behalf of the seven scattered around the world, I send you our thanksgiving. Whenever it must be, dear father, go in peace. You leave behind a tremendous inheritance, and sons and daughters still unscarred. Go, Dad. We will surely follow you.[6]

The secret of the blessed man. Your legacy. Your peace. Your hope.

Chapter 7

The Faith That Moves God
(A Military Person of Faith)

Matthew 8:5–13

Air Force Captain and F-16 pilot Scott O'Grady was shot down over Bosnia in 1995 while helping to enforce a NATO no-fly-zone policy. He was finally rescued after eluding enemy troops in the forests of Bosnia for six days. In his book, *Return with Honor*, O'Grady wrote, "That day, five miles up, with death at my front door, I found my key to life." He realized that only three things really mattered in life: faith in God, loved ones, and good health.

Like Captain O'Grady, our friend served in the military. We owe a great debt to him and to all persons who served their country faithfully. More important than his military service, however, was the fact that he knew what really mattered in life: faith in God and love of family.

Since the one we remember today was a person of faith, it is fitting to reflect upon some truths found in this passage from the Gospel of Matthew.

I. *A Person of Faith Is Affirmed by God*

First of all, a person of faith is affirmed by God. Jesus makes a remarkable statement about the centurion, a person in the military. He says, "I tell you the truth, I have not found anyone in Israel with such great faith" (Matt. 8:10). This assertion is truly amazing when you consider all the people the Lord met during his ministry.

Throughout the Scriptures, we see faith affirmed. In Jesus' parable of the talents, the Master affirms and rewards the servants who are faithful with the talents they were given. To the wise servants who increased their talents, the Master said, "Well done, good and faithful servant! You have been faithful with a few things; I will put you in charge of many things" (Matt. 25:21).

Jesus' parable of the talents in some ways reflects military life. For instance, a person faithful to duty at one rank gets promoted to a higher rank. Achieving rank in the military is crucial. But for the Christian service member, there's something even more important than getting promoted. And that is faithfulness to live the Christian life. The blessed irony is that devotion to Christ empowers a person to truly live by the essential values the military aspires to. [*The military values of the branch of the deceased could be* mentioned and/or reflected upon briefly here: Army: loyalty, duty, respect, selfless service, honor, integrity, personal courage; Navy: honor, courage, commitment; Air Force: integrity first, service above self, excellence in all we do; Marines: honor, courage, commitment.]

On May 12, 1962, General Douglas MacArthur gave an inspiring speech to the cadets of the U.S. Military Academy. He said, "Duty, honor, country: Those three hallowed words reverently dictate what you ought to be, what you can be, what you will be. They are your rallying point to build courage when courage seems to fail, to regain faith when there seems to be little cause for faith, to create hope when hope becomes forlorn."

MacArthur's speech refers to a kind of faith that is evident even when there seems to be little cause for faith. This perspective on faith is vital not only for Christians in the military but for Christians in all walks of life. We need to remember that it is not necessarily success (or what we normally perceive as success) that God affirms. God affirms the person who has faith and remains faithful regardless of the situation he faces.

The eleventh chapter of Hebrews records a faith "Hall of Fame." The heroes of faith are commended for having faith, but their situations don't all look the same. By faith, some conquered kingdoms, administered justice, gained what was promised, shut the mouths of lions, quenched the fury of flames, and escaped the sword. Others, however, were tortured, flogged, chained, put in prison, stoned, sawed in two, persecuted, mistreated, and put to death by the sword. So, one of the important truths we learn from

Hebrews 11 is that regardless of how things may seem, God still affirms faithfulness.

II. A Person of Faith Entreats God

A second truth from this passage is that a person of faith entreats God. In this story, the centurion came to Jesus with a plea. His faith was such that he believed Jesus had the power to save and heal his servant. Even though the Scriptures don't record the response, I would imagine the centurion rejoiced greatly when his servant was saved.

III. A Person of Faith Believes in God

A person of faith believes in God for salvation. That's the first step of faith: calling out to God and confessing our belief that Jesus has the power to save. By faith, we call out to God for redemption and forgiveness. "For it is by grace you have been saved, through faith" (Eph. 2:8). "'The word is near you; it is in your mouth and in your heart,' that is, the word of faith we are proclaiming: That if you confess with your mouth, 'Jesus is Lord,' and believe in your heart that God raised him from the dead, you will be saved" (Rom. 10:8–9).

On one hand, we grieve the loss of our friend; on the other hand, we rejoice that he had a saving faith. [*If known, the specifics of the person's salvation story can be mentioned here.*] Because of his saving faith, we take comfort in knowing that our friend has an eternal home, promised and prepared for him by God. In

2 Timothy 2, Paul speaks about being "a good soldier of Christ Jesus" (v. 3) and about the "salvation that is in Christ Jesus, with eternal glory" (v. 10).

IV. A Person of Faith Exhibits Goodness

A fourth truth is that a person of faith exhibits goodness. The centurion was worried about his servant, who was "in terrible suffering" (Matt. 8:6). He wanted to help his servant and called for Jesus to alleviate the suffering. This was the opposite of how masters normally treated servants in that day and age. It is an example of spiritual leadership—a military leader showing compassion and extending care to those under his authority. *[If known, a personal story portraying the deceased's spiritual leadership and compassion would be appropriate here.]*

In the movie *We Were Soldiers*, Mel Gibson portrays Col. Harold Moore, who, along with his troops, will soon deploy to Vietnam. Before they leave, a young lieutenant who was anxious about the deployment goes to the chapel seeking divine guidance. The colonel comes in and invites the lieutenant to go with him to the altar for a prayer. Neither of them knows what the future holds in Vietnam. Going before God in prayer together gives them encouragement and hope.

In his book *The Greatest Gift*, Henri Nouwen shares that one's faith is the greatest gift one leaves behind. By this, he is not saying that faith is inherited or passed on to others. Rather, a person of genuine faith lives and dies in such a way that family and friends who remain are left with a sense of hope and gratitude for the gifts of faith their loved one shared.

The Marines have a saying, *Semper Fidelis*, a Latin phrase which means "always faithful." Our friend was a person of faith: faithful to God, family, and country. We are grateful for his life and gifts of service. May our loved one's faithfulness serve as an inspiration for all of us in the life of faith, the key to life.

Chapter 8

The Sovereign of the Sudden
(A Sudden, Unexpected Death)

Mark 4:35–41

The Sea of Galilee is a sparkling jewel in the northern part of Israel. It is not large. It's more like a lake than what we think of as a sea. Only thirteen miles in length, seven and one-half miles at its widest point, surrounded by hills, including the Golan Heights, it was the chief source of revenue for its fishermen, of pleasure, and of beauty for those who lived around its shores. Jesus made his headquarters here. Many of his miracles and much of his ministry took place here. He called the early band of brothers, his disciples, from this area.

Seeking a break from the demand of the excited crowds that had begun to follow him, Jesus took a boat, and with some of his disciples, drifted off for some rest and relaxation. But suddenly their leisure day was disrupted by a violent storm. This was not unusual. The sea is 680 feet below sea level, surrounded by hills that send the cool air from the heights of Mt. Hermon hurtling through their ravines that serve as giant wind tunnels to collide with the warm, moist air flowing east from the Mediterranean Sea. The result can produce a very dramatic storm. In that sudden storm, Jesus did an astounding thing. And in that we learn some things that counsel us in the light of the devastating experience that we seek to navigate through in these days.

I. No Guarantee Against the Sudden

First of all, we are reminded that although the Sovereign of the universe is on the boat, it is no guarantee against the sudden—in this case, a sudden storm (v. 37). It has been the mistaken notion of many that if a person is a faithful follower of Jesus, he or she is protected from the troubles of life. Their children will be successful, sickness will never come their way, their financial ventures will always succeed, and disappointment will never knock at their door.

A quick look at some of the men and women who knew and served God in the Scripture will reveal the falsehood of this belief. Joseph went to prison. Job lost everything but his life. Jeremiah was put in prison. Paul had an affliction that plagued him all his life. All of the original disciples were martyred for their faith in Jesus, except one. And he was an exiled prisoner. Jesus never promised a "rose garden" tour of life. However, he did promise, "I am with you" (Matt. 28:20). It may be tough to be in a storm with Jesus, but imagine being in one without him.

II. It May Appear God Isn't Doing Anything

Second, it may appear that in these sudden experiences of life that grieve us and threaten our sense of God's nearness and care that God isn't doing anything (v. 38). These experienced, veteran fishermen were thoroughly frightened. Their lives were on the line, yet Jesus appeared to be sleeping through the situation.

In life, things come at us that we cannot control. Some things come through the actions of other people, and some things in life are never explained. God seems to be silent when we long for a word. One theologian, in facing this dilemma, said that "sometimes the silence of God is God's highest thought."[1] Like these hardy fishermen, we protest the seeming inaction of Jesus when he seems to be asleep at the wheel of our lives.

III. Fear Can Replace Faith

Third, we can respond like Jesus' disciples. Fear can replace faith. Jesus did hear their cries for help. He sprang into action. He spoke, and the winds ceased and the waves curled up around his feet like submissive tigers under the voice of their trainer. He then asked a penetrating question, "Why are you so afraid?" There are three words for fear in the language of the New Testament. Here Jesus used the one that is always used in a bad sense.

The men were deeply terrified. When fear comes, faith is removed. We live in a world with much to cause fear: the fear of terrorists, of illness, of losing our jobs, of being victimized by brutal criminals or white-collar fraud. Fear can immobilize us as it did

Jesus' companions. When fear knocks, we must send faith to answer the door. "For God hath not given us the spirit of fear; but of power, and of love, and of a sound mind (2 Tim. 1:7 KJV).

When the sudden comes in our lives, the Sovereign Savior is looking for us to look at him. They had seen Jesus do mighty things in recent days. They knew he had the power to heal the sick and cast out demons, but their faith trembled at this unexpected turn of events. In the light of his power and faithfulness in the past, Jesus asked, "Do you still have no faith?" (v. 40). Jesus challenges us to look deep within us and remember some things that can turn our pain, our grief, our questions, and our uncertainties into the beginning of healing in the face of this unanticipated event.

IV. Jesus Hears Our Cries

We are to remember that although Jesus did not hear the howling storm, he heard his disciples' cries. Much as a mother hears the cries of her baby and a shepherd hears the bleat of the sheep, so does Jesus hear our cries. "Surely the arm of the LORD is not too short to save, nor his ear too dull to hear" (Isa. 59:1).

V. Sudden Storms Serve to Turn Us to Jesus

Sudden storms also serve to turn us to Jesus (v. 38). We can be so caught up in everything else in life that God is moved into the edges of our existence. It doesn't happen quickly. But gradually the joy of knowing and serving him evaporates from our lives. Then the sudden storm hits. Before the storm we had forgotten what God looks like and now, in the storm, we turn to see him again.

VI. Storms Don't Last Forever

This story tells another helpful truth: storms don't last forever. In certain localities in this country and the world, as on the Sea of Galilee, a storm can brew within a matter of minutes and hurl its fury in torrents of rain, lightning flashes, and thunder. Then it's over. One minister said his favorite text was, "It shall come to pass" (Acts 2:17 KJV). So, too, will the turbulence through which we presently walk. The pain will linger, but its power will be softened.

VII. God Will Assist Others

The Sovereign of the Sudden does something else in our storms. He will assist others—who see us coming through our assault—to be blessed in the storms they are facing. When Jesus' boat started across the lake, "there were also other boats with him" (v. 36). They became survivors, too, because Jesus worked in the one and the overflow of protection encircled the others. People watch how we deal with our crises. Is God real in our lives? Is the faith we have practiced, sung about, and shared with others robust enough to take this blow?

A couple had prayed for a baby boy for years. God answered them after several childless years with a girl. A few years later, a boy arrived. But in his preschool years, he became violently ill one afternoon. He was immediately rushed to the hospital. The trauma team did their best. After a couple of hours, a doctor approached the mother with the news that the child's condition was critical. He would either die, or be physically disabled for life if, by slim chance, he survived. He turned to walk away while family and friends stood in stunned silence.

Suddenly, the mother called the doctor to come back. She said, "Doctor, thank you for what you've done. This child belongs to God. We prayed for him. God gave him to us. We gave him back to God. If God takes him, he's okay. If he leaves him, that's okay. If he chooses to take him, we're okay." And they were. And "other boats" were heartened by their experience.

VIII. The Sovereign of the Sudden Is in Control

Finally, storms remind us that the Sovereign of the Sudden is in control (v. 41). The disciples were overwhelmed by what they had seen. They had a new fear: a reverential fear. They had seen Jesus, with a word, rebuke wind and waves. They were reminded that the Sovereign of the Sudden is in control when everything else seems to be totally out of control. That boat could not sink because God's plan for the world was on it. Someone has said, "No water can swallow the ship where lies, the master of heaven, and earth, and skies."[2]

God's plan and purpose for our loved one and for our lives are not subject to whims, accidents, circumstances, illnesses, and evil. God works through these to bring about his will. We stand on the assurance, "Fear not, for I have redeemed you; I have summoned you by name; you are mine. When you pass through the waters, I will be with you; and when you pass through the rivers, they will not sweep over you. When you walk through the fire, you will not be burned; the flames will not set you ablaze. For I am the LORD, your God, the Holy One of Israel, your Savior" (Isa. 43:1–3).

David Watson was the dynamic pastor of the St. Michael's Church in York, England. Large crowds filled the sanctuary week after week to hear him call them to faith and fellowship with Jesus. In the prime of his life, Watson was diagnosed with cancer. The people prayed, and he fought it. But, in the end, it ravaged his body and he went home to the Chief Bishop of his soul.

The following Sunday, a cherished friend was asked to lead in the worship and the communion service. When he stood to speak, emotion overcame him as he thought of the absence of his recently deceased friend. He wept, as did the grief-stricken congregation. Then someone thought about a phrase that David often used. Sometimes, even in the middle of a message, Watson would shout, "Our Lord reigns!" Quietly, but strong enough to be heard, he said, "Our Lord reigns." Another picked it up. Then another joined them. Soon the packed sanctuary was filled with hundreds of voices, chanting together on their feet, "Our Lord reigns!" For minutes, it rocked the cavernous worship hall. Applause and cheering broke out.

Depression gave way to celebration. The Sovereign of the Sudden was, is, and always will be in charge. In our pain and sorrow, we stand on the everlasting truth, "Our Lord reigns!"

Chapter 9

When Our Why's Cause Us to Wonder
(A Tragic Death)

Judges 6:11–16

The question that bangs at the door of our hearts in the face of this tragedy is, *Why did God let this happen?* It is a question that we ask today and is one with which mourners have struggled through the ages. It is also a reality that draws people together. Someone has said, "Every worldview and religion is forced to deal with the issue of suffering. It cuts to the heart of our fragile existence . . . we are bound together by a bond stronger than social agendas. It is the bond of humanity and the suffering that marks us as a fallen people . . . it is the one experience that pulls at the soul of every person and dynamites the walls that divide us. We all meet and cry together at the smoldering ruins, the hospital, the funeral home."[1] It is a time to look for hope, to draw from Scripture and reason, and to experience some insight from this devastating experience of tragedy.

I. A Troubled Faith Is Better Than No Faith

We can be encouraged by knowing that a troubled faith in God is better than no faith. The judge Gideon in the Book of Judges was a perplexed man. He knew of God's mighty miracles. He had read and heard from his elders that God had delivered his people time after time. These stories were ingrained into his mind, but his current situation had led him to believe that God had not shown up. There was a keen sense of abandonment. He asked those questions we ask: "If the Lord is with us, why has all this happened to us? Where are all his wonders our fathers told us about?"

But faith reaches toward God, even though it may be a troubled faith. It's the faith on which Jim and Sally Conway stood when their daughter Becki faced an amputation: "The most important thing I learned is I only had two choices to make. One, to continue my anger at God and follow despair, or let God be God. I don't understand how all this fits together, the reasons for it, not even how to ask for an explanation. Despair or God, nothing in between, our family has chosen to hold on to God."[2]

II. God Is Not Obligated to Explain

Then we must understand that God is not obligated to explain. Scripture underscores this time after time. "It is the glory of God to conceal a matter" (Prov. 25:2). "The secret things belong to the LORD our God" (Deut. 29:29). "'For my thoughts are not your thoughts, neither are your ways my ways,' declares the

LORD. 'As the heavens are higher than the earth, so are my ways higher than your ways'" (Isa. 55:8–9).

It is in these times of silence that in some way the church becomes God's expression of love by reaching out with prayers, tears, embraces, acts of mercy, their presence, and whispers of encouragement.

III. God Is Not the Source of Our Heartaches

When our why's cause us to wonder, we realize that, in the final analysis, God is not the source of our heartaches. R. T. Kendall has stated that all of us are threatened by the "Betrayal Banner." It is his opinion that 100 percent of all believers eventually go through a period when God seems to let them down. It may occur shortly after becoming a Christian or when one's child becomes ill or when business reverses occur or maybe after seeing life start to unravel even though one has been a faithful believer for years. The natural reaction is, "Lord, is this the way you treat your own? I thought you cared for me, but I was wrong. I can't love a God like that."[3] Moses, one of the premier servants of God, voiced this kind of complaint to God: "Ever since I went to Pharaoh to speak in your name, he has brought trouble upon this people, and you have not rescued your people at all" (Exod. 5:23).

Faith can be hindered by a bitter experience. At times like this, we look at a source beyond ourselves: the enemy of God, his children, and his work. Who is that enemy? He is Satan, the one whom the Bible calls "the father of lies" (John 8:44), "a roaring lion looking for someone to devour" (1 Pet. 5:8), and "the accuser of our brothers, who accuses them before our God day and night" (Rev. 12:10). When that ancient foe whispers thoughts that make us distrust God and strike at our faith, we must stand against his false charges even though our faith trembles in the clouds of uncertainty.

IV. Sometimes God Delivers His People Through the Fire and Not From the Fire

We should also remember that sometimes God delivers his people through the fire and not from the fire. We are not exempt from calamity, nor should we expect to be. Jesus was perfectly clear when he said, "In this world you will have trouble. But take heart! I have overcome the world" (John 16:33).

One believer, having experienced a near-fatal car accident that resulted in a long recovery, several operations, and much suffering, received this insight as she recovered. Many people asked her, "Why did God let this happen to you?" She replied, "I tried to imagine a world in which God always delivers 'good' people from 'bad' things. I suppose God would have made the other driver's car suddenly sprout wings so that it would fly over our car without impacting. Or, perhaps, God should make it impossible for any driver to go through a red light and hit another car . . . in such a God-protected world, brakes would never fail on a car or truck. Airplanes would automatically be free of all defects—mechanical or those of the pilot or weather—especially if there were Christians on board. Christians would suddenly become very popular people if God gave special protection to them. You would want to be sure there was one in every plane, in every car, and, to protect from fire, in every hotel."[4]

If we get stuck on the *why?* we will never move forward. It's important at times like this to focus on what we have left, not what we have lost. Jesus lost his cousin and the one who announced him as the Lamb of God to a beheading by King Herod. When Jesus heard the news, he went to a solitary place to grieve. Then he returned and went back to his ministry of healing and teaching.

V. Trouble Rightly Handled Honors God

Next, when our why's cause us to wonder, we see that trouble rightly handled honors God. Jesus told a story about two men building houses. One built a house on a foundation of stone, the other on a foundation of sand. When the storms came against their houses, guess which one stood? When the cold, howling fierce winds of trouble and tragedy hurl themselves at the foundations of our lives, if we have built our lives on the Rock of Ages, the sure foundation, God can demonstrate valuable lessons to an observing world.

When Payne Stewart, Van Arden, Robert Fraley, and their friends and crew members were killed in the mysterious crash of their chartered jet several years ago, I was interviewed by one television reporter who had watched the amazing faith of their wives and families in the aftermath of the accident. His first question was, "Would you please tell us what these people have?" A vast number of people around the world were brought to faith or renewed in their faith as they observed the responses of courageous spouses in the face of heartbreaking tragedy.

VI. We Are Incredibly Precious to God

Another marvelous truth comes to us in these days: We are incredibly precious to God. "How precious to me are your thoughts, O God! How vast is the sum of them! Were I to count them, they would outnumber the grains of sand. When I awake, I am still with you" (Ps. 139:17–18). God's compassion to us is breathtaking. David states, "My tears are stored in your flask; are they not recorded in your book?" (Ps. 56:9 NAB).

When God walked among us robed in the flesh of Jesus Christ, he wept at the graveside of his friend, Lazarus, and over the citizens of Jerusalem. When one of his children passes from this life to eternity, what is his response? "Precious in the sight of the LORD is the death of his saints" (Ps. 116:15).

Charles Spurgeon penned these words to remind us:
God is too good to be unkind;
too wise to be mistaken,
When I can't trace His hand,
I must trust His heart.

VII. Our Faith Will Walk Us Through the Valleys

When our why's cause us to wonder, our faith must walk us through the valleys of doubt, despair, and discouragement. Someone has said that God is more interested in our faith than in our pleasure. Through the ages, he has used trouble and tragedy to deepen and strengthen our faith.

C. S. Lewis, who lost his wife to cancer shortly after they were married, wrote these words from his experience of grief, "You never know how much you really believe anything until its truth or falsehood becomes a matter of life and death to you."[5]

Author and pastor Max Lucado tells a wonderful story about his four-year-old daughter, Sara. Her favorite game was to jump into her father's arms. When she got him at just the right distance—not too close, mind you, but not too far away either—she crouched, sprang, and then threw her whole self at him. Superman without a cape. Skydiver without a parachute. Her only hope was her father. If he proved weak, she would fall. If he proved cruel, she would crash. If he should forget, she would tumble to the hard floor.

However, she didn't worry about any of that because she trusted her father. Four years under the same roof with him had convinced her that he was reliable. So she flew and soared, and he always caught her.

One day Sara's older sister was watching. Max asked Sara if she would jump to Andrea. Sara refused. Her father tried to coax her, but she wouldn't budge. "Why not?" he asked. "I only jump to big arms," she said.[6]

Our why's do cause us to wonder, but someday our why's will be answered and what is dark today will become light tomorrow. Vance Havner, wise evangelist of the last century, put it best: "When before the throne we stand in Him complete, all the riddles that puzzle us here will fall into place, and we shall know in fulfillment what we now believe in faith—that all things worked together for good in His eternal purpose. No longer will we cry, 'My God, why?' Instead, our 'Alas' will become 'Alleluia,' all question marks will be straightened into exclamation points, sorrow will change into singing, and pain will be lost in praise."[7]

God did respond to Gideon, "I will be with you" (Judg. 6:16). "God has nothing else to offer us. He does not answer our questions. Nothing to Gideon or us about the when or the how or the why; only the what, or even better, the *Who*. That is enough."[8] Jesus Christ, centuries later, reminded his followers before he left them, "And surely I am with you always, to the very end of the age" (Matt. 28:20). Our faith must rest on this eternal promise until our why's are answered and the light of eternity can illumine us.

Chapter 10

The Windstorms of Life
(A Suicide Victim)

God moves in a mysterious way,
His wonders to perform;
He plants His footsteps in the sea, and rides upon the storm.
Judge not the Lord by feeble sense, but trust Him for His grace;
Behind a frowning providence, He hides a smiling face.
Blind unbelief is sure to err, and scan his word in vain;
God is his own interpreter, and He will make it plain.
—William Cowper

Psalm 104:4

This hymn is one of many that were written by a man who had a record of long struggles with the drive to take his own life. William Cowper first attempted suicide when he was a young English lawyer. During a fit of madness, he tried to penetrate his heart with a penknife, but the point was broken. He then resorted to hanging himself with a garter, but it slipped off the nail.

After eighteen months in a "lunatic asylum" (as it was known in those days), he was released and became a friend of John Newton, the famous evangelical minister. Newton suggested they jointly publish a hymnbook. "Amazing Grace" became Newton's most famous contribution. And "God Moves in a Mysterious Way" became Cowper's best-known hymn. Cowper's majestic hymn was written after he went through the horror of another mental breakdown. At that time, he felt God demanded that he kill himself, like Judas, in order to hasten his final doom in hell. But he then rose out of the valley of the dark shadow to enjoy decades as the most popular poet of his eighteenth-century era. Even so, he ended his life in a mental institution, where he wrote his famous poem of despair, "The Castaway."[1]

In this hour of darkness and uncertainty, we look to the Scriptures to give us a measure of reassurance: "'With everlasting kindness I will have compassion on you,' says the LORD your Redeemer . . . 'Though the mountains be shaken and the hills be removed, yet my unfailing love for you will not be shaken nor my covenant of peace be removed,' says the LORD, who has compassion on you" (Isa. 54:8, 10).

I. Unexplainable?

In our grief and distress, we must acknowledge that suicide is unexplainable. To choose death over life goes against the tide of life that flows from the heart of our Creator God. Everything God touches brings life. We know that it is his will that we live.

Someone has written, "If there is God in it, it doesn't matter ever so little how we *feel* about it: it is an unbelievably precious and incalculable and endless thing."² But the nagging question of *why?* dogs our minds. If the question were answered and we knew the reason, the riddle would still be unanswered.

The family of the suicide victim carries a special grief. One mother whose teenage son took his life compared it to carrying a book bag loaded with boulders. The book bag may be filled with regret one day, feelings of failure the next, and guilt the next. But no matter what's in it, the book bag always weighs her down. Family, we offer our prayers, love, and support as you begin to reshape your lives.

Guy Delaney framed it for us this way: "What questions can we ask and what answers can we expect? Some questions we hesitate to ask for fear of the answers we may get, and some answers we give are worse than no answers. Any one of us might give the answer that was given to a Frenchman who, at the turn of the century, went to a physician and said, 'Doctor, you've got to help me. I can't go on with life. Please help me end it all.' And the doctor said, 'Now, now, my friend, you mustn't talk that way. You must laugh and smile and enjoy life. Make friends. Mix with people. Why not go to the circus tonight and see the great clown Debereau. He will make you laugh and forget your troubles.' The man looked into the face of the physician with his sad eyes and said in a painful whisper, 'But doctor, I am Debereau.'"³

II. Unusual?

As we struggle with our questions, our inadequacies, we may be overcome with the sense that maybe we failed at some point. We may be overcome with anger and guilt. We must sadly admit that, although we do not know all the circumstances surrounding this death; unfortunately suicide is not unusual.

We say not unusual because of biblical, historical, and contemporary records. There are seven recorded instances of suicide in the Bible. Every year approximately two million people attempt suicide, and fifty thousand are successful. Every minute someone tries to self-destruct. Five thousand youth succeed.[4] The highest suicide rate is among the elderly. Suicides occur most frequently in the spring and holiday seasons, on Thursday, among Protestants. Three or four times as many men as women take their lives in this country.[5]

In the face of this, how must we respond? We, the living, have responsibilities to the fellow citizens of our community of life. One thing we can do is not to be judgmental. We do not know what causes a person to resort to taking his own life. It can be burdens about which we had no knowledge or overwhelming tension, anxiety, failures, unresolved guilt, loneliness, or the relentless attack of our ancient adversary, Satan, whom the Bible calls our accuser. It can be a chemical imbalance that, for a period of time, causes reason to be replaced, mental control to be lost, and judgment and the stronger sense of pursuing life to be snapped.

We must be compassionate and understanding. We should be sensitive to the cries for help that surface in our families, friends, and colleagues. If someone mentions suicide to us, we should take it seriously. We should express genuine interest in their problems, listen carefully to such phrases as "I'm thinking about checking out" or "I'm just tired of living." Don't argue, act quickly to get them to professional Christian counsel, and pray for them and with them. These simple things can be the difference between life and death. We should humbly remember as one has written: "We are all so much more fragile than we know—because what we feel and do can hardly be understood apart from our past and present life circumstances . . . we must all bear in mind, 'There, but for the grace of God, go I.'"[6]

III. Unforgivable?

What about the question of suicide's being the unforgivable sin? The church had little to say about it in the early centuries, but Augustine, in the fourth century, asserted that suicide was a sin. By A.D. 563, the church prohibited funerals for any suicide, regardless of the circumstances, and by 1284 refused suicide victims burial in a consecrated cemetery.[7] Theologian Thomas Aquinas, in the thirteenth century, wrote that it was the worst sin of all because you could not repent.

What say we? Is suicide a sin? Yes. God gives life. "I have come that they may have life, and have it to the full" (John 10:10). Unpardonable or unforgivable? No. A person can destroy the body, but not the spirit. The Bible is clear that we go either to heaven or hell based solely on our relationship to Jesus Christ. "Because of his great love for us, God who is rich in mercy, made us alive with Christ even when we were dead in transgressions . . . For it is by grace you have been saved, through faith—and this not from yourselves, it is the gift of God" (Eph. 2:4–5, 8). We believe, as Scripture so firmly assures us, that all who have trusted Jesus Christ can never be separated from his eternal love.

Do you think anyone is going to be able to drive a wedge between us and Christ's love for us? There is no way! Not trouble, not hard times, not hatred, not hunger, not homelessness, not bullying threats, not backstabbing, not even the worst sins listed in the Scripture . . . None of this fazes us because Jesus loves us. I'm absolutely convinced that nothing—nothing living or dead, angelic or demonic, today or tomorrow, high or low, thinkable or unthinkable—absolutely *nothing* can get between us and God's love because of the way that Jesus our Master has embraced us (Rom. 8:35–39 The Message).

IV. Unshakable?

In the midst of our questions and grief over this distressing and complex heartache, we turn our hearts to the supreme truth: We have a Savior who, in troubling times, is unshakable! Walter Winchell was a famous radio news commentator during

World War II. Once, after a particularly dark week during which the port of Singapore fell, he closed his broadcast with this sentence: "Singapore has fallen, but the Rock of Ages stands."[8]

This is the time—when we walk through this windstorm of life—that we find our footing in the shifting sands of emotional feelings and mental anguish by looking to Jesus who promised, "Peace I leave with you; my peace I give you. I do not give to you as the world gives" (John 14:27).

We stand on God's Word in times like this, for his Word . . .

Teaches us the greatest truth,

Offers the greatest good,

Meets the greatest need,

Holds out the greatest hope.[9]

Chapter 11

Grief: A Season We Must Embrace
(One Who Battled a Long Illness)

1 Peter 1:6

A pastor received a letter from a fellow minister who lived in the nation of Kenya. It read, "I only know God's faithfulness in filling the void that is left when a beloved one is taken from us. I am saddened by the passing of my late wife. The pain and grief is still very real, and it is a season that we must embrace."[1] Grief is very real. It can begin early in life with the loss of a pet, a stolen bike, or the death of a grandparent. Its sting is unique.

In his book *A Grief Observed*, C. S. Lewis relates the feelings of grief as he watched his wife's slow death from cancer. The opening words of the book are: "Nobody ever told me."[2] Grief's impact is universal. It stalks every home, knocks at every door. Rich and poor of every race in every nation know the reality of grief and tears.

The Bible speaks of grief eighty-eight times and of tears forty-five times. Jesus Christ, the Lord of life, was a man acquainted with sorrow. He wept over the death of his friend, Lazarus, and over the lostness of the city of Jerusalem. Bible heroes walked the corridors of grief: Jeremiah, Peter, Jacob, Joseph, Ruth, Hannah, David, the early church.

Peter writes to a scattered band of believers who have been removed from their houses, familiar communities, possessions, and jobs. Now persecution has set in on the church as he writes these words: "In this you greatly rejoice, though now for a little while you may have had to suffer grief in all kinds of trials" (1 Pet. 1:6). As he dealt head-on with grief, so must we.

You have walked a long time with suffering. You have prayed. You have wept. You have hurt. Let us seek to begin the healing process.

I. Respond

We all must respond to grief in this season we must embrace. Grief can hide under many masks, but it must be exposed and guarded against. It can be a feeling of guilt or anger, like Martha. She reproached Jesus as he came to her home at the death of her brother Lazarus: "If you had been here, my brother would not have died" (John 11:21). It can come in waves of depression. It can be buried in a host of busy-ness and activity. It can even be denied. But it must be handled.

II. Remember

We embrace our grief by remembering. This loss must be reviewed. Hang on to it long enough to allow its full effect to settle in your soul. Our contemporary society says move on, fix it quick. But in biblical tradition and history, people took time to grieve. Jesus did when he heard of the terrible death of his cousin, John the Baptist. "When Jesus heard what had happened [to John], he withdrew by boat privately to a solitary place" (Matt. 14:13).

"Forget those who say that grief is a sign of lack of faith or that only weak people grieve. Grief is natural and God, in his wisdom, has provided us an outlet for dealing with our sorrow and pain. Remember. Cherish the memories. Tears of joy will come, as well as tears of sadness. The funeral service is not the middle or the end of grieving. It is just the beginning."[3]

III. Rebuild

Then, we must rebuild. The questions that have tumbled through your minds and echoed in the chambers of your heart— How long will this take? Why is this happening? Where is God in all of this?—are normal questions.

Robert Ozment relates the story of a young woman in his church whose husband was killed in a plane crash. He asked her to write some thoughts about the time of grief immediately following his death. After months, her answer came: "For the first few days, I lived with the question: Why, God? Then that question dropped and I began asking, Which way, God? God never answered the first question, but he did answer the second one. The first thing was a sense of gratitude for the years God gave my husband and me together. Then, I knew life had to go on. My mother taught me that as long as there was life, we had a responsibility to God and others. All of us hurt on the journey of life, but it would be wrong to pull down the shades and shut the door. Finally, I was sustained by the presence of God. He was with me as I stumbled down the lonely road of sorrow. I have come through the dark night and felt the touch of his hand."[4]

First, we rebuild by asking the Lord for his help. "In my anguishI cried to the LORD, and he answered by setting me free" (Ps. 118:5).

Second, we rebuild by understanding that grief is the price we pay for the ability to love. "The joys of yesterday are more than enough for the sorrows of tomorrow."[5]

Third, we rebuild by the awareness that there is a tomorrow. Tony Campolo relates a funeral service he attended for a twenty-year-old man in west Philadelphia. The preacher took the first fifteen minutes reviewing the promises of the resurrection. He walked down to the family and spoke words of comfort. Then he did an unusual thing. He turned to the open casket and began to address the deceased. He thanked him for his life and his faith. When he finished the litany of memories, he said, "That's all I have to say except, "Good night, Clarence, good night!" He slammed the lid on the casket, turned to the congregation with a smile and said, "But I know God is going to give Clarence a good morning!" With that, the choir started singing, "In that great gettin' up morning, we shall rise, we shall rise!"[6]

Finally, we rebuild by standing on the promises of God. "He will wipe every tear from their eyes. There will be no more death or mourning or crying or pain" (Rev. 21:4).

We have another promise given to us through the inspired pen of Paul: "We can tell you with complete confidence—we have the Master's word on it—that when the Master comes again to get us, those of us who are still alive will not get a jump on the dead and leave them behind. In actual fact, they'll be ahead of us. The Master himself will give the command. Archangel thunder! God's trumpet blast! He'll come down from heaven and the dead in Christ will rise—they'll go first. Then the rest of us who are still alive at the time will be caught up with them into the clouds to meet the Master. Oh, we'll be walking on air! And then there will be one huge family reunion with the Master. So reassure one another with these words" (1 Thess. 4:15–18 The Message).

Someone has said, "Paul did not seek to comfort the bereaved with platitudes culled from the philosophers—he did not mock their grief with verses from the poets, leaving them heavy of heart in empty habitations. He just reminded them that their dead had taken a short journey to a glorious land, and that their trip was to be a round trip! In terms of calm finality that was rooted in an unimpeachable source, he told them that Jesus was coming back to reign over his earth and that, when he came, he would bring their dead with him!"[7]

Grief is real. It is a cleansing river for the soul. God has wired us emotionally to come to grips with our loss and embrace our grief. This is a time of processing. Its purpose is to bring healing that we might continue to live significantly. "'For I know the plans I have for you,' declares the LORD, 'plans to prosper you and not to harm you, plans to give you hope and a future'" (Jer. 29:11). Grief is a season we must embrace so we might move, strengthened, into the future.

Chapter 12

Coming Late to Jesus
(A Recent Convert)

2 Chronicles 33:1–20; Matthew 20:1–16

One of baseball's legends, Mickey Mantle, was a hard-driving athlete on the field and a hard-drinker off the field. Later in life, he had a liver transplant. As he was recovering, he stated to reporters, "It seems like all I've done is take. Have fun and take." Asked if he had signed an organ donor card, he replied, "I don't have anything good to give. Everything I've got is worn out. I've heard a lot of people say they'd like to have my heart (because) it's never been used. God gave me a body and an ability to play baseball. God gave me everything and I just . . . " He then stopped in mid-sentence and gestured as if throwing it away.[1]

Mickey Mantle had wasted his life in many ways, but something good happened to him late in life. A baseball-playing buddy led him to faith in Jesus Christ. Mickey came to faith late, but he came. That's a word of hope. That's the God of the Bible. This amazing truth is highlighted throughout Scripture to remind us of the wideness of God's mercy and the kindness of his justice.

Two accounts from the Bible underscore this reality. One is from the Old Testament. King Manasseh of Judah ruled in Jerusalem for fifty-five years. He led the people to worship false gods. He consulted witches and mediums. He put other carved idols in the temple. He even sacrificed his sons to the gods of the pagans.

Later in his reign, Manasseh was taken into captivity. There God did a work in his heart. "In his distress, he sought the favor of the LORD his God and humbled himself greatly before the God of his fathers" (2 Chron. 33:12). And God's response? "The LORD was moved by his entreaty and listened to his plea; so he brought him back to Jerusalem and to his kingdom. Then Manasseh knew that the LORD is God" (2 Chron. 33:13). God welcomes latecomers!

The other story is a parable that Jesus shared with his disciples. It was set in the labor market. As in many cities today, there was a labor pool. Persons needing some extra hands could find them there. It was grape harvest time, which is usually in September in Israel. The crop had to be harvested quickly. The owner hired a number of workers early in the day for one silver coin each—not much money, but enough to feed your family for a day. The owner returned three hours later and hired more for the same price. He repeated this at noon, again at 3 P.M., and then at 5 P.M. Then the owner did an incredible thing. He settled up with his workers that night, paying everyone the same thing. Some grumbled and complained, but the owner had kept his word. Jesus added one unforgettable sentence to the story. The kingdom of heaven is like this. "The last will be first, and the first will be last" (Matt. 20:16).

This story and the story of Manasseh teach us many timeless truths relevant to the person whose passing you grieve today.

I. God Initiates the Process of Conversion and the Call to Service

The first timeless truth is that God initiates the process of conversion and the call to service. We come to Christ only by his sheer grace. Someone has said, "Without Christ we are homeless . . . Beware of those who are homeless by choice."[2] All of us are homeless until we are at home with Christ.

Homecomings and reunions are a part of the fabric of our lives. High school, college and church homecomings, as well as family and class reunions bring a special joy to us. Even more so to God. The prodigal son illustrates this. A young man was sick of home, then he got homesick, then he came home again.[3] God calls all of us to come home.

II. God Is Generous

The second truth is that God is generous. It has been said that God is good to everyone in some ways, and to some in all ways. James put it this way, "Every good and perfect gift is from above, coming down from the Father of the heavenly lights, who does not change like shifting shadows" (James 1:17). Put in today's language, God loves to give first-class upgrades!

III. God Had Rather Forgive Than Judge

The third truth that leaps out at us is that God had rather forgive than judge. God is indeed holy, righteous, and the ultimate judge of all mankind. But he is also forgiving, merciful, and loving. Many people miss this side of God's character.

A woman shared the following story in an interview on television. She grew up an atheist, had attended no church, and had uttered no prayers. At the age of thirty-six, she heard the news that her daughter was in a serious car accident and, perhaps, in a coma that would last for years. To cope with her anger and grief, the woman went to a bar, drank heavily, and got into her car to go home. Rain was pouring on her windshield as the wipers tried to keep up with the downpour. She pulled to the side of the road, turned off the engine, and began to curse God. For half an hour all the venom of a lifetime spilled out as she finally had the courage to tell God what she thought of him. When she finished, there was dead silence. Then she heard a voice: "This is the first time you have talked to me . . . I love you."[4]

IV. God Rewards Quality as Much as Quantity

A fourth truth emerges for latecomers. God rewards quality as much as quantity. He reestablished Manasseh as king. He gave to those who had worked only one hour the same as those who had worked for twelve hours. His love does not calculate the "less or more."[5] He is not a *quid pro quo* operator. He owes us no explanations for what seems to be unfair. He does not answer all of our questions about suffering, hardship, and difficulties. In the end we must affirm with Ralph Waldo Emerson, "All I have seen teaches me to trust the Creator for all I have not seen."[6]

V. God's Companionship Is Our Compensation

The fifth truth is that, in the final analysis, God's companionship is our compensation. For Manasseh, even though he had little to give back to God, "he got rid of the foreign gods and removed the image from the temple of the LORD, as well as all the altars he had built on the temple hill and in Jerusalem; and he threw them out of the city. Then he restored the altar of the LORD and sacrificed fellowship offerings and thank offerings on it, and told Judah to serve the LORD, the God of Israel" (2 Chron. 33:15–16).

The workers in the vineyard? Even though some came late, they not only were paid fairly, but they had the privilege to work for a while and to serve the owner. Although the journey of service to Jesus Christ may be short, it can be wonderfully precious.

Steve Brown tells of his relationship with his wife, Anna: "In college, when Anna and I first dated, I didn't have money or a car. To pay for college, I ran a laundry. Other guys had plenty of money and took their dates to the theater and out to dinner, while we just walked around campus and held hands. I said to Anna, 'I wish I could afford to take you out.' She said to me, 'I don't care where we go, as long as I'm with you.'"[7] The ultimate compensation is companionship with God through Jesus Christ our Lord.

God's desire is that we come to him. It is better to show up late than not at all; better at sunset, than never. When we come, we find the faithful, forgiving Savior ready to welcome us into his home and family.

Steve McQueen was an actor who led a life as tough as those he portrayed on screen. Success filled his life until alcohol and a failed marriage left him empty. In despair, he attended a crusade led by one of Billy Graham's associates. McQueen made a profession of faith and requested an opportunity to speak with Billy Graham. A connecting flight in Los Angeles allowed Graham to speak a couple of hours with McQueen in the actor's limousine. The great evangelist shared numerous passages of Scripture in his attempt to give spiritual hope and confidence. Steve McQueen struggled with the thought of God's giving eternal life to a man who had such a sinful past.

Finally, in Titus 1:2, Steve McQueen found his promised hope: "The hope of eternal life, which God, who does not lie, promised before the beginning of time." He requested something on which to write down the verse, but Graham gave McQueen his Bible instead.

Steve McQueen died in Mexico while seeking experimental treatment for his terminal cancer. He passed into eternal life with his Bible opened to Titus chapter 1 and his finger resting on verse 2. Regardless of our pasts, we have the hope of God's eternal promise.[8]

We are forever grateful that for this loved one it was not too late to experience the grace and mercy of Jesus Christ. "This is how God showed his love for us: God sent his only Son into the world so we might live through him" (1 John 4:9 The Message). It has been said that the important thing is not when, but that we came.

Chapter 13

The God of the Second Chance
(One Who Returned to the Faith)

Luke 15:11–32

You may recall being homesick. It could have been that first night away from home as a child, leaving for college, or being in another country and missing home.

Another kind of homesickness is experienced spiritually. Initially it is the awareness that God has "set eternity in our hearts" and the longing to know him personally.

When faith is placed in Jesus Christ as our Savior, we come home to our Lord and Creator. After that initial homecoming, some wander away from him. They become a "prodigal." Webster defines a prodigal as a person who wastes his means.

The Bible has several stories about prodigals: Samuel and his two sons, David and Absalom, and the one prodigal son in the parable that Jesus told. A parable illustrates truths about the kingdom of God. Called most often "the parable of the prodigal son," this story could also have been called "the parable of the compassionate father."

In this story we find a contemporary dilemma—one that takes place in many homes. The prodigal experience is not isolated to the non-Christian world. It happens in the best of Christian homes. Because this parable is so relevant to all cultures in all generations, it brings insight, assurance, and hope for all of us today.

This story can be divided into three parts. The first part (vv. 11–12) reveals the youngest of two sons requesting his part of the family inheritance. Jewish law designated that two-thirds of a man's goods were to go to the principal heir, the oldest son in this case, and one-third to the second son. The normal procedure was that it was to be given at the death of the father. The younger son's request was unusual, but the father gave him his portion.

The second part (vv. 13–20a) describes the experience of the runaway. He runs far from home. His lifestyle is extravagant. In time, his resources erode and he finds himself in difficult circumstances. He goes from living "high on the hog" to living *with* the hogs! He becomes a broken, devastated man. He is far from home. He is lonely and desperate. He begins to evaluate his life. Is he hungry? Yes. Is he isolated? Yes. Did he know there was assistance at home? Yes. What sent him home? Two hungers: one in his stomach and one in his heart. In the harsh reality of barrenness, he knew there was an oasis of hope and help at his father's house. He prepares a speech. It expresses true brokenness. The prodigal

The God of the Second Chance

is humble. He doesn't ask for any favors—just a place of work and, hopefully, of forgiveness.

The third part of this story, often regarded as the greatest short story in the world, describes his journey home (vv. 20b–24). His heart has preceded his feet, but not his father's compassionate concern. Every day since his departure, the father had been scanning that road on which his son had departed. Finally, the father sees a familiar figure. While the walk is slower and the figure more slumped than his son's when he left, this father knew beyond what he saw that this was the son he had temporarily lost. The father rushes down the steps to the sweat- and sand-covered figure. And then he did something unusual for Jewish fathers. He ran. For a Jewish man who wore long robes, running was a humiliating thing. But not on this occasion. Decorum was cast aside. And joy, hugs, kisses, fast-flowing words were the order of the day.

The son manages to get his repentance speech out, but the order of the day is celebration. A ring was given to the son to signify sonship, sandals were given to represent family position (as slaves went barefoot), and a robe was given to symbolize the exalted place of an honored guest. A fatted calf was prepared for very important guests—and this son was such a guest. The party begins.

The God of the Second Chance has rolled out the welcome sign for this son whom he loves. This famous story is really a handwritten letter from God to teach us lessons about him and us as prodigals.

I. Prodigals Can Appear in the Best of Families

From this parable, we learn the lesson that prodigals can come from the best of families. Sometimes that is difficult to handle for the parents or family of one who has been raised in a Christian home, and for the church when they seemingly turn their backs on God and family. But it is true. And we can learn God's wisdom in this. The father in the parable did not panic. We must always remember that God is in control. "We know that in all things God works for the good of those who love him" (Rom. 8:28). We are also reminded that we should not inflict false guilt on those we love who wander away from God.

There are no perfect parents. We know that Adam and Eve had a perfect Father in a perfect environment, but they chose to rebel against God. Statistics tell us that 60 percent of teenagers who leave home were not physically, sexually, or mentally abused. They just took off. Husbands and wives can be in a solid marriage and one begins to wander. Faced with this situation, we must always remember that prodigals bear the responsibility for their choices—not the parents.

II. We Must Refuse Bitterness

Then, we must refuse to become bitter. The wasted resources, years, and experiences as well as the unanswered questions can easily lead to a bitter spirit in the parent. However, the prodigal's father did not react bitterly to his son. Paul reminds us, "Get rid of all bitterness, rage and anger" (Eph. 4:31). We replace bitterness with forgiveness.

Buddy Scott, in his book *Grief for Hurting Parents,* relates the following helpful exercise. Let's imagine that your child rebelled against you, left home, and journeyed to a distant city beside the sea to get away from you to live his defiant lifestyle. You get your yacht and tie a huge barge to the back of it. Then you take all your grudges out of your heart—the ones you've been stockpiling and warehousing—and pile them on the barge.

And off you motor in your yacht, towing your garbage barge behind you. You're headed toward your child's seaside city to tell him off, to show your garbage collection to him, and to make him realize what an ungrateful little wretch he has been.

The longer you pull your garbage barge, the more it begins to stink. You notice that it has begun to affect you inside as you catch yourself secretly rehearsing how you will tell him off. You notice that your whole family is suffering from the anger and resentments you have piled up. You've even begun to notice physical symptoms of the unsanitary burdens.

You set your brow and scream, "But I don't feel like cutting my barge loose! Look at that pile of garbage! I deserve to be mad! I'm going to pull this barge up to my kid and throw him in his own garbage! He's going to know how badly he's hurt me!"

The pull is long and hard. You have time to think. There's a bad storm brewing. The diesel engines groan. You're running low on fuel. Your frustration factor is at an all-time high. The stench is getting worse. Your family is hurting. Suddenly, the truth dawns: "I had better get rid of this garbage or it's going to get rid of us!"

You ask yourself, "What do I really want, anyway? Do I want to prove how 'bad' my son is, or do I want him rescued and safe?"

You answer, "I want him back." Then you wonder, "Well, what good is this garbage barge?" And it hits you. "Will this thing heal? Jesus wouldn't be pulling a garbage barge behind him to show someone how contemptible he is. The Bible says that he came to us not to condemn us but to redeem us."

You walk to the back of your yacht with knife in hand. You stare at the garbage on your barge. You're still hurt, and you don't feel like letting go of your grudges. But Christians don't go by feelings. They go by wisdom. Putting wisdom over feelings, you reach down and cut yourself free. The barge drifts to a stop, and you leave it behind. It vanishes in the golden triangle of God's mercy, grace, and forgiveness. You're no longer a garbage collector.[1]

III. We Must Have Unconditional Love

Another thing we learn is unconditional love. Three times in this story, the word *compassion* is used. It's a word that expresses deep inner feeling, a real down-in-the-soul deep. It does not reflect on what the past and difficult circumstances have cost us. It is proactive and speaks clearly of how much I love you. The more love we give, the more like Jesus Christ we are. "Everyone who loves is born of God and experiences a relationship with

God" (1 John 4:7 The Message). The God of the Second Chance never ceases loving and being willing to forgive.

IV. We Should Cling to Persistent Hope

We also see the power of persistent hope. The father never gave up. He believed his son was coming home. He was prepared for that eventuality by having the calf ready for the party. He was looking down the road. He would not be shaken from this earnest belief.

G. F. Watt painted a famous painting entitled "Hope." It pictures a poor woman against the world. Her eyes are bandaged so that she cannot see ahead. In her hands is a harp, but all the strings are broken—save one. Those broken strings represent her shattered expectations, her bitter disappointments. That one last unbroken string is the string of hope. She strikes that string, and a glorious melody floats out over the world. It fills her dark skies with stars. The artist painted a great truth. Even when all else is gone, you can still have hope.[2]

The God of the Second Chance doesn't waste our prodigal days. With him there are no wasted sorrows. When a person ends up in the far country, he may ask, "What's the meaning of this, God?" And God patiently waits until we humbly ask that question.[3] People can be at the top of the ladder, successful in every way the world judges as successful, and still be a prodigal. But they can also go home again.

Greg Laurie tells of a cat named Clem, who one day decided to leave home. After a while his owners sadly concluded that they would never see Clem again. Eight years later they heard a scratching at their door. They opened it, and in walked a cat they didn't think they had ever seen before. He climbed up into Clem's favorite chair and started purring as if he owned the place. They thought, *Could this be Clem?* They found old photographs of their cat from eight years ago and compared them to the cat in the chair. Sure enough, it was Clem. How did he find his way home? Where had he been? What kept him away? No one will ever know. But he had some kind of homing instinct and found his way after a long time.[4]

Isn't it amazing that God has placed this homing instinct in all his children? In the long run, whatever time may have ticked off on the prodigal clock, the prodigals will realize that everything they have ever needed or wanted was in the Father's house and they can come home again.

That's what salvation is all about. It's about coming home to God and having an eternal home with him and enjoying an everlasting love. In salvation, he cuts the trash away and dumps it in the river of grace to be swept away and remembered no more.

Everyone who has ever dealt with a prodigal can relate to the prayer from the musical *Les Miserables*. In this prayer, the father cries out to God for his son. As he prays, he repeatedly asks, "Bring him home, let him live."

This beloved one is forever home. Safe in the arms, the everlasting arms of the God of the Second Chance. Prayers were heard. Prayers were answered. We celebrate the joy of their return and the expectation of reunion in the Father's house.

Chapter 14
Life's Dimensions
(Evangelistic)

Psalm 90:1–12

[*Begin by reading Psalm 90:1–2.*] This prayer of Moses, a great man of God, is a comfort and a challenge to you today. Your grief and loss is real. You're placing this death event into your view of life and eternity. What better way to find focus than to look at our everlasting God and his message of life and hope.

Moses leads us into the many facets of time and eternity with the everlasting God as the all-encompassing life, from here through eternity.

I. Life's Context

First, we note life's context (vv. 1–2). Moses reminds us of the big picture of life and eternity: "From everlasting to everlasting you are God" (v. 2). To acknowledge God, who is, who was, and who will ever be is, difficult for our finite minds. God has no beginning and will have no ending.

When we take our life and place it against the backdrop of eternity, it causes us to reevaluate what we are doing, what we believe, to whom we are committed, and for what purpose we are here on this earth. Because you are seeing your life against the backdrop of eternity, you are able to make better choices. Galatians 6:7 declares, "Whatsoever a man soweth, that shall he also reap" (KJV). The choices you are making determine the crop that you will harvest.

Here is another reason it is good to look at life from the backdrop of eternity. The focus of you alongside and against the backdrop of the everlasting Father will bring you into a spirit of humility. It is difficult to be filled with the pride of life and the haughty spirit of self's greatness when you place yourself in backdrop of the eternal God. We have a tendency to be filled with pride of accomplishment and greatness of personhood.

Jesus would remind us: "Learn from me, for I am gentle and humble in heart" (Matt. 11:29). What is your placement of life today? Use these moments in reevaluation and placement against the backdrop of our God, who is from everlasting to everlasting.

II. Life's Brevity

Second, we note life's brevity (vv. 4–6). A teacher once stimulated her students to think about life and its brevity by placing the figure 25,550 on the board for them to see when they arrived for class. Soon one of the students asked the teacher why that number was there. She explained that the number represented the number of days in the life of a person who lives to be 70. And, since most of you in this room have lived 16 years, 5,840 days are gone, and only God knows how many days you will have in this brief journey on earth.

In Psalm 90, Moses uses the picture of grass growing up in the day, being impacted by the noonday sun, then slowly withering by evening. So life appears as grass growing and withering (vv. 5–6).

James depicts life as "a mist that appears for a little while and then vanishes" (James 4:14). Today is all you have. Yesterday is past. Tomorrow may not come. So, today, recognize that time is precious. In your todays, speak words of love to family, encouragement to fellow employees, kindness to the less fortunate. Do good to others in your todays. Restore broken relationships. Heal misunderstanding and confusion. Bring peace to troubled waters. Share with someone the good news of Christ and his wonderful love. Do these things in your todays.

The great preacher of a past era, Jonathan Edwards, wrote, "I resolve to live with all my might while I do live. I resolve never to lose one moment of time to improve my use of time in the most profitable way I possibly can. I resolve never to do anything I wouldn't be doing if it were the last hour of my life."

III. Life's Difficulties

Third, we note life's difficulties (vv. 9–10). Into every life comes troubles, illness, stress, sorrow, and confusion. Moses underscores that no one is exempt from life's difficult moments. He describes them as being marked by "trouble and sorrow." But, throughout Scripture we are told that God is the one who comes alongside to bear your burdens, comfort your sorrow, and lead you through the difficult journey.

Jesus promised the holy Comforter. He said, "I will not leave you comfortless, but I will come alongside to lift you up through life's difficulties and challenges" (John 14:18, paraphrase). Do you sense the Comforter ministering to you today? He promised he would come. So receive his presence and grace, his love and strength for your present need.

IV. Life's Decisions

Fourth, we note life's decisions (vv. 10b, 12). Moses helps us focus on the spiritual dimensions of life. We have been reminded that God leaves us free to choose our directions of life. A prayer by an unknown saint should be ours in these times:

Teach me, O Lord, not to hold on to life too tightly.
Teach me to hold it lightly; not carelessly, but lightly, easily.
Teach me to take it as a gift, to enjoy and to cherish while
    I have it.
And to let go gracefully and thankfully when the time
    comes.
The gift is great, but the Giver is greater still.
Thou, O God, are the Giver and in Thee is a Life that never
    dies. Amen.[1]

Moses stated it so simply, "Teach us how short our lives really are so that we may be wise" (Ps. 90:12 NCV). In your todays, it is wise to decide to follow God. Moses knew the impact of a life devoted to God and his ways.

In the New Testament, we read the words of Jesus: "I have come that they may have life, and have it to the full" (John 10:10). Jesus would say in John 14:6, "I am the way and the truth and the life. No one comes to the Father except through me." He would go on to say in John 11:25–26, "I am the resurrection and the life. He who believes in me will live, even though he dies; and whoever lives and believes in me will never die." You are wise when you make the conscious decision as an act of your will to receive Jesus as personal Lord and Savior. He is willing that none perish, but that all come to repentance.

As Moses has written, "God has always been and God will always be" (Ps. 90:2, paraphrase). We, too, live forever. So this decision for Christ is crucial because eternity is at stake. If you are "in Christ" at death, you go to live with him for eternity. But if you have rejected Christ, then at death you are separated from God for eternity in a place called hell. But Jesus died on the cross and paid for all your sins so that if you trust him and him alone for your salvation, then you will have everlasting life with him forever.

How do you do this? Simply turn to Christ, confess your sins, and ask him to forgive your sins. Then as an act of your will—in faith, believing—ask Christ to come into your life, to forgive your sins, and to save your soul forever. The moment you ask him, you become a child of the King. When you die some day, he will take you home to heaven.

Today is the day of salvation. Do not harden your heart against life's most important decision.

Chapter 15

The Unchangeable Promise of Jesus
(Evangelistic)

Luke 23:39–43

The hope of the heart is to live in a meaningful existence beyond the brief span of time on the place we call earth. This is seen in the growing interest in freezing the body after death so that when a cure for diseases is found, the body will be thawed, illness cured, and the individual can continue the process of life. Others are hoping that medical science will allow their DNA to be cloned so that they can be duplicated in a kind of constant reincarnation. Some are praying that a new pill or drug will slow the process of aging and life can be extended indefinitely. The reality is that all of us will die sooner or later. The Scriptures tell us the truth: "Man is destined to die once, and after that to face judgment" (Heb. 9:27). The questions are, Where will the spirit spend eternity? With whom? And how does one make the essential arrangements?

When Jesus was in his last hours before his death on the cross for the sins of humanity, he was crucified between two thieves. Perhaps Pilate wanted to insult this man who claimed to be a king by hanging him between these criminals.

But God had his reasons for allowing this crucifixion that went far beyond Pilate's intentions. God, in his providence, allowed two thieves to frame Jesus' cross with their own. This was their opportunity to go to heaven. One took it. The other refused.

In the unfolding drama of the cross, the story of the one who cried out to Jesus for mercy is probably one of the most surprising and instructive incidents in all the Gospel narrative.[1] It is a story of faith and hope, as well as a glimpse at the unchangeable promise of God on which we stand in our common sorrow. As the repentant criminal turned to Jesus, we see a man who was willing to be saved, a man who confessed the innocence of Jesus: "This man has done nothing wrong" (v. 40). We see a man who recognized the deity of Jesus when he asked to have a share in his kingdom. And we see a man of faith. His words, "When you come into your kingdom" (v. 42), are riveting. Not "if," but "when!" Here was a man who stormed heaven with his dying breath.

Jesus' reply brought him dying grace and brings us living instruction, confidence, and promise. The words? "Today you will be with me in paradise" (v. 43).

I. Destroys the Idea of Annihilation

In the unchangeable promise that Jesus gave the thief, we learn that Jesus destroys the idea of annihilation. Death is the separation of two basic elements of man, the material from the immaterial, the spirit from the body. Life is the union of soul and body. Death is the disassociation of the two. "Then shall the dust return to the earth as it was: and the spirit shall return unto God who gave it" (Eccl. 12:7 KJV). Death in the Bible does not mean extinction, but separation. Physical death does not put an end to man's existence. It changes the nature of that existence.

II. Denies the Lie of Soul Sleep

This unchangeable promise denies the lie of soul sleep. Well-meaning people teach that the spirit, at death, lapses into unconsciousness until the resurrection. In the New Testament death is called "sleep." When Jesus was informed of the death of his friend Lazarus, he said, "Our friend Lazarus has fallen asleep; but I am going there to wake him up" (John 11:11). Paul said, "To be absent from the body, and to be present with the Lord" (2 Cor. 5:8 KJV).

Paul wasn't yearning for death so he could have a long sleep. He anticipated it because he knew he was going to be with Christ immediately after his physical body had quit functioning. When Jesus promised the repentant, dying thief that he would be with him in paradise, Jesus said, "*Today* you will be with me in paradise" (Luke 23:43, emphasis added).

III. Declares There Is No In-Between State

Next, this unchangeable promise from Jesus declares there is no in-between state where the spirit hovers in a kind of limbo, awaiting an uncertain fate, dependent upon some kind of intervention—human or divine—to move it into heaven. There is no biblical evidence to support this theory. It did not exist in the Christian church until medieval times.

IV. Demonstrates the Delight of Heaven

Finally, this unchangeable promise of Jesus demonstrates the delight of heaven. Heaven means different things to different segments of society. For some religions it is to be in the company of beautiful virgins; for others it is a vapory-like existence; for still others it is symbolic. For those who trust the Scriptures, it is a real place, a source of inspiration, an incentive for living, a comfort, and a ballast.

Will exchange time for eternity. What does Jesus' promise to the thief mean to us today? It means we will exchange time for eternity. Time is a probationary period filled with the tools of tears and disappointments. Eternity with Jesus is a settled state with progress and complete knowledge. "We don't yet see things clearly. We're squinting in a fog, peering through a mist. But it won't be long before the weather clears and the sun shines bright! We'll see it all then, see it all as clearly as God sees us, knowing him directly just as he knows us!" (1 Cor. 13:12 The Message).

Will realize the promise of a new home. We presently live in a world of refugees and homeless. But the believer in Christ will have a new home called paradise. The word *paradise* is used only three times in the New Testament. It means an enclosed park or pleasure ground.

In 1888, thirty-three-year-old George Washington Vanderbilt III set out to build the grandest home in America. He purchased large parcels of land near Asheville, North Carolina, including the 100,000-acre Pisgah Forest. He commissioned two of the most distinguished architects of his time to design this superstructure and the surrounding grounds called the Biltmore Estate. It was designed to be a four-story edifice with a 780-foot facade. The construction called for over one thousand workers. Marble was imported from Italy. Thirty-two thousand bricks were made on the site daily.

On Christmas Eve, 1895, Vanderbilt unveiled his prized Biltmore Estate. It boasts 4 acres of floor space, a total of 250 rooms, 34 master bedrooms, 43 bathrooms, 3 kitchens, 65 fireplaces, an indoor swimming pool, and a gymnasium.

Despite its opulent grandeur, even the Biltmore Estate pales in comparison to the architectural accomplishments of Jesus Christ in heaven. In the unseen world above, Jesus is building a mansion that will overshadow anything ever built by human hands."[2] "'No eye has seen, no ear has heard, no mind has conceived what God has prepared for those who love him'—but God has revealed it to us by his Spirit" (1 Cor. 2:9–10).

Will recognize and be recognized. We also have the unchangeable promise of Jesus that we will recognize and be recognized in heaven. Charles H. Spurgeon once remarked, "We knew one another on earth. Will we be bigger fools in heaven?"[3] Jesus promised, "I say to you that many will come from the east and the west, and will take their places at the feast with Abraham, Isaac and Jacob in the kingdom of heaven" (Matt. 8:11). Those ancient heroes of the faith will be in heaven, and they will maintain their same identity.

Judson B. Palmer relates a story told by A. D. Sanborn, who preceded him as pastor in a church in Iowa. Sanborn visited a young Christian woman who was seriously ill. She was bolstered up in bed, almost in a sitting position, looking off in the distance. "Now just as soon as they open the gate, I will go in," she whispered. Then she sank upon her pillow in disappointment. "They have let Mamie go in ahead of me, but soon I will go in." Moments later she spoke again, "They let Grandpa in ahead of me, but next time I go in for sure." No one spoke to her and she said nothing more to anyone, and seemed to see nothing except the sights of the beautiful city.

Later in the day, the pastor learned that the young woman had died that morning. He was so impressed with what she said that he asked the family about the identity of Mamie and Grandpa. Mamie was a little girl who had lived near them at one time but later moved to New York state. As for Grandpa, he was a friend of the family and had moved somewhere in the southwest.

Sanborn then wrote to the addresses given him to inquire about the individuals. Much to his astonishment, he discovered that both Mamie and Grandpa had died the morning of September 16, the very hour that the young woman herself had passed into glory.[4]

Will be in his presence. Then we have the unchangeable promise of Jesus that we will be in his presence: "With me." Someone has said that all of heaven is in those last two words. Salvation and heaven is a person before it's a place.

In the catacombs of Rome, where early Christians entombed their dead, you will find many symbols, signs, and words of hope concerning that reality. One of these says, "He went to live with Christ."[5]

Matthew Huffman was the six-year-old son of missionaries in Salvador, Brazil. One morning he complained of a fever. As his temperature went up, he began losing his eyesight. His mother and father put him in the car and raced him to the hospital. As they were driving, Matthew did something his parents will never forget. He extended his hand in the air. His mother took it, and he pulled it away. He extended it again. She took it again and he pulled it back once more and reached into the air. Confused, the mother asked her son, "What are you reaching for, Matthew?" "I'm reaching for Jesus' hand," he answered. And with those words he closed his eyes and slipped into a coma from which he would never awaken. He died two days later, a victim of bacterial meningitis.

Although he did not learn many things in his short life, he learned the most important: who to reach for in the hour of death.[6]

Two thieves were being executed along with Jesus that day. One knew who to reach for, the other didn't. One found Jesus' hand. The other found an eternal death separated from the Savior forever. Death for the believer is not stepping into an alien atmosphere; it is going home. Not an empty home, but a home in the presence of Jesus forever. Everyone should make the wise decision of the repentant thief, and reach for the saving hand of Jesus.

In our sorrow and grief at death, for death is an enemy, we are comforted with the unchangeable promise of Jesus: "I tell you the truth, today you will be with me in paradise" (Luke 23:43). God's Word urges us, "Today, if you hear his voice, do not harden your hearts" (Heb. 4:7).

Chapter 16

Looking the Enemy in the Face
(General)

1 Corinthians 15:50–58

Stonewall Jackson was one of the most renowned and revered generals of the Civil War. He was known as Robert E. Lee's "right arm." Shortly after leading his army to a memorable victory, he was accidentally wounded by "friendly fire" one fateful night. The initial wounds were not fatal, but infection and pneumonia set in and the death watch began. Shortly before he died, Jackson, a devout Christian, raised himself to ask the attending physician, "How do I look in the face?"

Facing death, as all of us do, we also may ask, "How do I look in the face?" The early Christians, just as with every generation, had many questions about death. *What happens to our bodies?* The apostle Paul wrote one of the greatest chapters of hope in the Bible about facing death. Paul's words encouraged Christians in that day and they speak to us today. *What does God have to say to us in the face of the ancient enemy called death?*

I. Death Is Inevitable, but Not Natural

God says, "Death is inevitable, but not natural."

According to one of the tales of the old West, there was a character named Wild Bill Langley. He supposedly had killed thirty-two people. He became a legend because on one occasion he was strung up to be hung by vigilantes. They began to shoot at him as he swung by the rope. They missed him, hit the rope, and he escaped. On another occasion, a sheriff tried to hang him, but made the rope too long and Wild Bill dropped to his feet on the ground. Some people felt that since he had cheated death so often, his casket was filled with rocks, and he had escaped. They dug up his grave to see if he was really there. The DNA matched that of his descendants. Wild Bill didn't cheat death. No one does. We cannot cheat it, but we can defeat it. Through Christ we can move from death to a larger life.[1]

Scripture reminds us of the reality of death: "Man is destined to die once" (Heb. 9:27). Death is the most common event in human history. More common than marriage, because not everyone marries. More common than child-bearing because not all men or women have children.

The tragedy of death is that it was not a part of God's original plan. He created man to live, not to die. God is the life-giver. Everything he touches brings life. Sin entered the arena of life through the first man. And death has been on the scene ever since.

As human beings, we try to give meaning to death. Some do it by seeking to be master of it by trying to control their destiny through suicide or euthanasia. Others seek immortality through the false hope of reincarnation. There are others who do it by trying to leave a legacy, a memorial of their lives, through the family, manuscripts, works of art, or other achievements. But there is no cure for death.

Faced with this reality, the question arises, "Where is God in the face of death?" Uncertainty about the future can lead to many things.

- For the psalmist, it led to distress: "The cords of death entangled me, the anguish of the grave came upon me; I was overcome by trouble and sorrow" (Ps. 116:3).
- For some, it leads to a sense of despair: "Are the dead a live audience for your miracles? Do ghosts ever join the choirs that praise you? Does your love make any difference in a graveyard?" (Ps. 88:10–12 The Message).
- For others, it leads to paralyzing fear. The writer of Hebrews writes of those who "all their lives were held in slavery by their fear of death" (Heb. 2:15).

II. God Is Involved, Not Passive

God is involved, not passive in the face of the cries of our humanity. He becomes involved with us as we face the king of terrors—death. Psalm 116:15 assures us, "Precious in the sight of the LORD is the death of his saints" (KJV).

When we face the chilling waters of death, God begins to work in our lives. Several things happen. First, God has our full attention. Then he reminds us that he has walked with us through other dark valleys and he is prepared to help us in this one. As he guides us through, he can unwrap some of the things he has in store for us. In John 14:2 he promises, "I am going there to prepare a place for you."

What kind of place is heaven? The apostle Paul tells us: "No eye has seen, no ear has heard, no mind has conceived what God has prepared for those who love him" (1 Cor. 2:9). Have you ever had the experience of moving into a new house or having someone show you through theirs? Just imagine the Lord's showing us through the place he has prepared for us!

Because we go to heaven, it gives the opportunity for others, touched by our influence and testimony, to come to Jesus. In God's economy, it seems that the only way for some people to go to heaven is for others whom they know, love, and respect to go before them. The desire of their hearts is to see them again. And because of this desire, the door of salvation is opened. We can be sure that God is not passive. He works in life and through death.

III. Death Is Intimidating, Not Triumphant

As we look the enemy in the face, there is one other thing of which we can be assured: Death is intimidating, not triumphant. It is not the ultimate visitor. Paul's words shout at us in these victory words in 1 Corinthians 15:50–58. *[Read Scripture at this point.]*

There is life beyond this world. Life extends beyond the physical. There is more to come. Because of the resurrection of Jesus Christ, all who belong to him will live forever. Jesus put death to death. Because he did, we go from termination to emigration.

The following words were found on the ancient tombstone of a Christian: "The inn of a traveler on his road to Jerusalem." Winston Churchill, the famous prime minister and war leader of England during World War II, was buried at the Blandon churchyard. These words are written on the gate as you leave the cemetery: "I know that my Redeemer liveth."

How do I look in the face? When we look into the face of Jesus Christ as our Savior and Lord, we can say as Paul did: "'Where, O death, is your victory? Where, O death, is your sting?' Therefore, my dear brothers, stand firm. Let nothing move you . . . Always give yourselves fully to the work of the Lord, because you know that your labor in the Lord is not in vain" (1 Cor. 15:55, 58).

Chapter 17

Journey to the Father's House
(General)

Psalm 23:6

In Florence, Italy, is one of the world's most treasured art works: Michelangelo's eighteen-foot-tall statue of David. The work is so well crafted, that you would not be surprised if it started moving and speaking. The renowned artist captured some of the essence of this man whose influence has spanned three thousand years. David was a military genius, a political leader, a superb musician, a poet of renown, and, above all, a man obsessed with God. Psalm 27:4 underscores this obsession: "One thing I ask of the LORD, this is what I seek: that I may dwell in the house of the LORD all the days of my life, to gaze upon the beauty of the LORD, and to seek him in his temple."

David was truly "a man after God's own heart." His heart for God had its origin in his youth. The Twenty-Third Psalm captures this preoccupation. This psalm is loved by all, and many people think it was written in David's youth. However, it was probably the capturing of his thoughts at the end of his life. He reflected on his days as a shepherd boy. And in those beautiful memories, he speaks to us about the next step in the life journey of a child of God: going to our eternal home. He sees the shepherd as good—not only for our past, not only for our present, but for our future.

I. Assured of God's Promises

First, we are assured of God's promise. "Surely" is a statement of faith, a statement of assurance. Certainty means everything when the difficulties of life surface; when the job folds up; when our child doesn't get in the school to which we had applied; when we look in the mirror and realize our bodies are bending south; when the "zero" hours come and everything in life is turned upside down; when the lean seasons come and life seems like more dead ends than through streets; when, like Paul, "we were harassed at every turn—conflicts on the outside, fears within" (2 Cor. 7:5), we need his "surely."

The glorious reality is we have God's promise, and "not one of all the good promises the LORD your God gave you has failed. Every promise has been fulfilled; not one has failed" (Josh. 23:14). He has assured us of a place: "There is plenty of room for you in my Father's home. If that weren't so, would I have told you that I'm on my way to get your room ready for you? And if I'm on my way to get your room ready, I'll come back and get you so you can live where I live" (John 14:2–3 The Message).

II. Accompanied by God's Pilots

In that trip to join the Good Shepherd, we are accompanied by God's pilots: "goodness and mercy." What is God's goodness? It's the sum total of all his attributes. It is his character, the very nature of God. "The LORD is good to all" (Ps. 145:9). There is a common goodness to all, and a special goodness to his children. Someone has explained that "God is good to all in some ways and to some in all ways."[1]

What is God's mercy? *Mercy* means "loving-kindness, tender affection." In the ancient world, it was a love that flowed with deep emotion—even to those who were dishonorable, despicable, and unworthy. These two pilots of life do an amazing thing. They "follow me"—which is a war word, a military term that means "relentless, tireless, doggedly."

David knew what it meant to be pursued. Much of his life had been spent on the run. And now he turns it into a positive picture. These guardian angels become a heavenly escort. Kyle Yates explains, "These twin angels of God will never sleep, never fail, never prove inadequate. They are a part of the provision of a loving God who has determined to give personal, individual help at every moment all life through."[2]

III. Aware of God's Presence

Then, we are aware of God's presence "all the days" of our lives. These brilliant angels walk before us, behind us, around us as constant companions, pointing us unswervingly toward home.

Ken Taylor, who is known for his paraphrased version of the Scripture known as The Living Bible, was asked to write an autobiography of his life. He hesitated for a while, then consented. In his prologue, he stated, "It is the story of an ordinary life with some extraordinary events scattered through it. I fear it is not the exciting reading that some autobiographies are, though I have experienced some dramatic highlights that I will tell you about. It is the story of God's quiet leading, sometimes into exciting events, but more often in day-by-day living. Many years ago, when I left the work I loved so much at Moody Bible Institute, leaving job security to work full-time translating The Living Bible, I knew I was taking some risks with the welfare of my large family. I recall remarking with deep feeling to my oldest son, 'I'm not sure where I am going, but I know it will be a guided tour.' And of course I meant guided by God. And so it has been, just as I believed."[3] God's presence is with us in the present for sure, but there's also a future tense.

IV. Abides in God's Place

Lastly, we have an abiding place. "I will dwell in the house of the LORD forever." What did David mean by 'the house of the LORD? "It couldn't have been the temple in Jerusalem, because it wasn't yet built. And it wasn't the house he wished to build for the Lord, because he used the word 'forever' and noman-made house lasts forever. "No, it was something far greater than a house or a temple. It was another *life*. "It was an eternal home."[4] God intends for us to be home with him forever. We are never fully home here on earth. Everything is temporal here.

C. S. Lewis relates this idea to his conversion experience. "I have come home at last . . . this is my real country! I belong here. This is the land I have been looking for all my life, though I never knew it until now."[5]

That eternal home is established by a personal relationship through faith in Jesus Christ. For the believer, that comes at a certain point in life and continues forever. Death cannot stop it.

In the best-selling book *Tuesdays with Morrie*, writer Mitch Albom tells of one of his last conversations with his college professor, Morrie. Morrie said, "It's natural to die . . . Everything that gets born dies; do you accept that?"

"Yes."

"Here is the pay-off. Here's how we are different from plants and animals. You live on—in the hearts of everyone you have touched and mastered while you were here . . . Death ends a life, not a relationship."[6]

When faith is placed in Jesus Christ, our relationship with him as his children continues right on through our entrance through the doors of death when we will be ushered into the presence of our Father. That place is called heaven. Heaven is to be in the presence of Jesus.

"The Amplified Bible brings out the sense of this last sentence when it states, 'Through the length of my days the house of the Lord [and His presence] shall be my dwelling place.' Not only do we get the idea of an ever-present Shepherd on the scene, but also the concept that the sheep wants to be in full view of his owner at all times . . . from the sheep's standpoint it is knowing that the shepherd is there; it is the constant awareness of his presence . . . providing a sense of security and serenity."[7] What a place it must be!

The Taj Mahal was prepared as a monument of love. It was built between 1632 and 1653 by Shah Johar for his wife. Constructed of white marble, it glistens like a jewel on the bank of a wide river. The exterior is inlaid with black onyx in flowing script depicting quotes from the Koran; the interior, including walls and ceiling, is inlaid with semiprecious stones in floral designs. The Taj Mahal was intentionally designed not as a palace or as a summer residence, or even an elaborate bathhouse. The Taj Mahal is a tomb! It was built by the lavishly romantic and wealthy shah for his beloved wife, to whom he'd been married for only fourteen years, when she was overtaken by the great equalizer—death. In writing about this, Anne Graham Lotz continues, "If one Indian ruler could prepare something as breathtakingly beautiful as the Taj Majal as a tomb for his wife of just fourteen years, what must God be preparing as a home where he will live forever and ever with His people whom He loves?"[8]

"No one's ever seen or heard anything like this, never so much as imagined anything quite like it—what God has arranged for those who love him" (1 Cor. 2:9 The Message).

Glen Payne, a member of the famed Cathedrals gospel singing quartet, suffered a losing bout with cancer and went to be in the presence of his Savior. His wife, Van, reported how he left this world. He would come in and out of consciousness and look wide-eyed toward the ceiling and around the room as if he was looking into eternity. He said, "Wow! Wow!" Over and over again Glen would say "Wow!" When he finally passed away, he was singing, "What a Day That Will Be." When he got to the part, "When he takes me by the hand," Glen took his last breath on this earth.[9]

There's only one way into the Father's house. Jesus said, "I am the door: by me if any man enter in, he shall be saved, and shall go in and out, and find pasture" (John 10:9 KJV). For any of you who have never begun the journey, you are invited to join us. For those who are on the journey, be encouraged. The best is yet to come!

Chapter 18

On the Other Side
(General)

John 14:1–6

Do you remember this prayer?
Now I lay me down to sleep,
I pray the Lord my soul to keep;
If I should die before I wake;
I pray the Lord my soul to take.

Children have been praying that prayer for centuries. It may be the first prayer you remember praying other than the meal-time prayer:

God is great,
God is good,
Let us thank him for this food.

Even as a child, the former prayer moved your thoughts from this world to another world: a mysterious world, a world framed by time known as eternity—a world that, for people of faith in Jesus Christ, is called heaven. When those we know and love pass from this world to the next, it moves us to seriously contemplate the place where they have gone. Our eyes and ears are more focused when the clutch of death claims those who have been such a significant part of our world.

I. Existence

We think about the existence of heaven. Is there really such a place? A poll taken by CNN in recent years found that 81 percent of the American public believes there is a place called heaven. This is unusual in that there are so many things to interrupt our thinking and planning for the next world. One Christian theologian called it "the dimming of heaven." Our belief in heaven has been dimmed by materialism—distorted and fantasy views of materialism, the push to make ends meet, and a this-world-only mentality. But the Bible mentions heaven 550 times. Twice Jesus called it a "place" in John 14:2–3. It is a location. It translates the Greek word *topos* from which we get our word *topography*. It is not a state of mind. It is not an abstraction. It is not a foggy, wishful sentiment. When Jesus taught us to pray what we commonly call "The Lord's Prayer," he did not say, "Our Father, who art in a state of mind or condition."[1]

What is heaven like? After defecting to the United States, Orestes Lorenze Perez knew he had to rescue his family from Cuba. So one Saturday afternoon, flying low in a borrowed Cessna to avoid radar, he swooped down into Cuba, past his former neighborhood, and landed in traffic on a coastal road. His family ran to the plane, and they were soon leaving the Cuban shore, en route to freedom.

His wife, Victoria, had waited patiently. But it was hard. Going to America seemed to her like going to "heaven": "When I saw the plane, I screamed to my children. 'That's your father!' I grabbed both of them and we ran," she said. As they ran, one of the kids lost a shoe. "Forget the shoe!" Victoria screamed. "Father is in the plane!"

After two years of separation, the family had been reunited. To Victoria and Orestes, their new home in America is like heaven: a place of freedom, a place where they can realize their dreams.

For Victoria, America had been a vague reality. She knew her husband was there and it would be better there, but she had few details to make it real in her heart. For us, heaven is often vague. As America was for Victoria, heaven remains a distant dream.[2] But God in his wisdom and grace gives us some perspective for life on the other side.

II. *Experiences*

When we become convinced by the authority of Scripture and the promises of God that there is a heaven, what are some of the experiences of the other side? In the *Family Circus* cartoon, the older sister is pictured reading a book that looks like a Bible to two of her younger brothers. She states, "Heaven is a great big hug that lasts forever."[3]

Heaven is difficult for us to comprehend because no human has ever been there and back to tell us about it. Some have made it so unrealistic by speculation about sensual pleasure, nature themes, or even endless perfect rounds of golf on a championship course. Questions do arise in our mind. They are normal. For some of them, Scripture does give us insights.

Possibly the question that is most frequently asked is, Will we know our loved ones and one another in heaven? In a number of places, Scripture indicates the answer is yes. One of these is at the Mount of Transfiguration. Peter, James, and John immediately recognized Moses and Elijah, even though both had lived nearly one thousand years before them (Mark 9:1–5). In the story of the rich man and Lazarus (Luke 16:19–31), the rich man could remember, reason, talk, communicate, and even feel concern.

The apostle Paul, writing to the believers in Thessalonica, describes heaven in these terms: "For what is our hope, our joy, or the crown in which we will glory in the presence of our Lord Jesus when he comes? Is it not you? Indeed, you are our glory and joy" (1 Thess. 2:19–20). Paul expected to see and recognize those he had led to faith and discipled. He expected them to recognize him. Since we know one another here, can we not expect to know more completely when we are made perfect?

And, oh, yes, the Bible records that we will have a name in heaven: "The general assembly and church of the firstborn, which are written in heaven" (Heb. 12:23 KJV).

Will we be married in heaven and continue in the relationship we have known on earth? This is not a new question. Jesus dealt with it when he was questioned by religious leaders who asked him about a woman who had outlived seven husbands. Whose wife would she be in the resurrection? Jesus' reply, an important one as it is recorded in three books of the Bible, was clear. "Those who are considered worthy of taking part in that age and in the resurrection from the dead will neither marry nor be given in marriage, and they can no longer die; for they are like the angels. They are God's children, since they are children of the resurrection" (Luke 20:35–36).

We go to heaven as the children of God. We'll be career singles but we are in a family. In heaven, we will have a perfect family. Our relationships will never be strained; there will be no disruption, no bitterness, no disagreements. We will live in perfect harmony in the family of God.

People have often wondered what age we will be in heaven. Will we be the same age as we were at the time of our death on earth? Does a baby grow up? Does a teenager get an adult body? Does a senior body, crippled by age and disease, get retrofitted with a youthful body? It has been suggested that we will be the same age as Jesus when he finished his assignment on earth and ascended into heaven. That seems to be reflected in these words: "But we know that when he appears, we shall be like him, for we shall see him as he is" (1 John 3:2). We cannot verify that, but we can be sure that there will be no age in heaven as age implies aging. There will be no growing older in heaven. "For the perishable must clothe itself with the imperishable, and the mortal with immortality" (1 Cor. 15:53).

Some people wonder if we will be able to see what's going on in planet earth from heaven. There is no evidence that this is true, but neither can it be ruled out. Erwin Lutzer tells of a seven-year-old girl in the Moody church who asked her father, "Can we ask Jesus to get a message to Grandpa?" He was caught somewhat by surprise but realized there was nothing in his theology that would cause him to say no. So he responded, "Yes, that might be possible; let's tell Jesus what we want Grandpa to know."

We might not be sure whether Jesus gave the message to Grandpa, but we must agree that this little girl's theology was better than that of millions of other people in the world. She knew that although we might pray to Jesus to get a message to Jesus, those in heaven cannot communicate with us.[4]

III. Exceptions

There will be nothing to mar the joy of heaven. There will be no remodeling, recalls, repentance, reprimands, resentments, revenge, or regrets in heaven. C. S. Lewis once suggested that if hell could inject regret into heaven, it would mean that hell had won after all.[5] Heaven is perfection. Everything God does is complete and exquisite.

We do know there are some things God will not allow on the other side. We might call them the exceptions. Revelation 21:4 tells us what is absent in heaven. Death is gone. Tears are gone. Crying is gone. Pain is gone. Sin is gone. It is totally absent. Gone are murderers, unbelievers, those who are sexually immoral, sorcerers, idolaters, and liars. There will be no sun or moon. Jesus Christ and the Father are the luminaries (Rev. 21:23). There is no night there—nothing to eclipse the light of the universe or shadow his splendor. There will be no curse on the other side. That which has troubled mankind from early in creation will be lifted, never to trouble us again.

IV. Essence

But the very essence of the other side is to see Jesus face-to-face. Revelation 22:4 says, "They will see his face." Have you ever wondered what Jesus looked like? Ever wondered what it would be like to be near the King of glory? Moses asked to see God, but God did not reveal his face to Moses. God said, "You cannot see my face, for no one may see me and live" (Exod. 33:20). But on the other side, we will have that face-to-face privilege to see our eternal Father. In the circle of time encased in the circuit of eternity, we will behold him.

The important question for every living person is, How do I get to the other side, to heaven? The world offers many roads, but Scripture points out only one way: "I am the gate; whoever enters through me will be saved" (John 10:9).

James Dobson tells about talking to his seventeen-year-old son, Ryan, about the sudden death of their friend, Pete Maravich, one of basketball's greatest players. Pete came late to Christ, but he came strong.

We must all face death sooner or later in one way or another . . . Sooner or later you will get the kind of phone call Mrs. Maravich received today . . . I don't know if I'll have an opportunity to give you my "last words" so let me express them to you right now. Freeze frame this moment in your mind and hold on to it for the rest of your life. My message to you is be there! Be there to meet your mother and me in heaven. We will be looking for you on that resurrection morning. Don't let anything deter you from keeping that appointment . . . his is the only thing of real significance in your life. I care what you accomplish in the years to come, and I hope you make good use of the great potential the Lord has given you. But above every other purpose and goal, the only thing that really matters is that you determine now to be there![6]

The "other side," where Jesus Christ is awaiting us, is glorious. Don't miss it. Take comfort that because of him and his sacrificial death on the cross, there's more—much more—to come.

Chapter 19

Assurance for Troubled Days
(General)

Psalm 121

Many have experienced the adventure of putting up a tent or shelter of some kind in the backyard during childhood days. It was a time of beginning to grow up. Sometimes a friend would camp out with you—sometimes a brother or your dad. But most of the time, you wanted to experience it by yourself. As the night deepened, the sounds and shadows began to take on ominous meaning in your mind. Your imagination would soar as fear and uncertainty began to find a niche in your armor of bravery. A brewing storm, with rising winds, flashes of lightning, and the rumble of thunder were sure reasons to look for help. It was always an assurance to see the lights go on in the house and your mom or dad call out to see if you were okay. The door was always open to come inside under their loving care and the protection of the father's house.

As life progresses and we enter the adult world, there are heartaches, troubles, grief, and sadness that send our hearts on a search for assurance, for shelter in the storms that swirl through every life. In this hour of sorrow and trouble, we look to God's Word for guidance and strength.

Psalm 121 has been a treasure chest of assurance for centuries. Its writer is anonymous. The exact time or place of its writing are not indicated. It was one of the "Psalms of Ascent." These psalms were sung by religious pilgrims as they made their way to Jerusalem to observe sacred holidays and feasts. The city of Jerusalem is surrounded by hills, giving it an appearance of strength and refuge. But the pilgrim psalmist had insights on a deeper level. His comprehension was far more vertical than the 2,800-feet-above-sea-level peaks that punctuate the skies above the city of David.

I. Cause of Assurance

First, in this psalm we see the cause of assurance (v. 1). The traveler knew well the hazards of the journey. Weather, robbers, murderers, lack of adequate food or housing, and illness awaited him. The insecurities of life are intimidators for us, as well. Many people live in mortal fear and feel they are hostage to the unexpectedness of life and evil. Fear, that internal warning cry of trouble ahead, grips our lives.

What are we to do? One version of the Bible translates this verse to read, "I will lift up mine eyes unto the hills, from whence cometh my help" (KJV). The better translation includes a question mark, "Where does my help come from?" And then the psalmist answers his own question. It is not in the hills—as magnificent as they are. They are helpless to aid in his hour of need. He looks to the Creator of the hills, not the creation. "My help comes from the LORD, the Maker of heaven and earth" (v. 2). The Master Designer, the God who has created 800,000 cataloged insects, billions in some species, is the one who stands by us. Our abilities are inadequate, but we know the God who is more than adequate to sustain us in our day of trouble.

II. *Certainty of Assurance*

Second, we are encouraged by the certainty of assurance (vv. 3–6). "He will not let your foot slip" (v. 3). An old hymn underscores this truth. "How firm a foundation, you saints of the Lord, is laid for your faith in his excellent Word." Christ is our solid rock. Notice his presence on our behalf. Six times in six verses, the words *watch* and *keep* are used. Ten times the Lord is referred to. Ten times the second person suffix is used. God is alert to every trouble. He does not abandon us. He is not asleep on the job.

Lloyd Ogilvie, respected pastor and former chaplain of the United States Senate, tells of meeting with an adult group at his church in California. The meeting was held in the home of dear friends. To express a warm welcome to their pastor, they kept a place open in their driveway for his car. A beautiful, gothic-lettered sign read, "Please reserve for Dr. Ogilvie." After Ogilvie's talk and prayer time with the group, his host offered him the sign to take home.

The next morning he left home early for a breakfast meeting, but had a humorous idea. His wife, Mary Jane, was still asleep. He crept back into the house, went to their bedroom, and, without waking her, put the sign and the stand in his place in their king-sized bed. When she made the bed after breakfast, she found the sign and called him at the office with laughter in her voice. She had some nice, affectionate things to say about the fact that she was glad that the place in their bed was reserved for him.

Later, after a night in which he found it difficult to sleep because of some concerns, Mary Jane added eight words to the sign and put it in the bed while Ogilvie showered the next morning. When he returned to the bedroom there it was: "Reserved for Dr. Ogilvie to sleep, trusting the One who never sleeps!" He had tried to take over the Lord's responsibilities.[1]

The psalmist reports that God not only watches over us, but he is our "shade" (v. 5). Often in Scripture we find the word-picture of shade to symbolize God's presence. Psalm 17:8 says, "Hide me in the shadow of your wings." In Isaiah 51:16 we read, "I have . . . covered you with the shadow of my hand." Psalm 91:1 assures us, "He who dwells in the shelter of the Most High will rest in the shadow of the Almighty."

In verse 6 the phrases about *the sun* and *the moon* remind us of God's protection day and night, 24/7. *The right hand* (v. 5) speaks of "the primitive practice of the protector of a king or leader whose assignment was to always stand at his right hand to ward off attacks and to hold the armor and weapons ready for battle."[2] The bottom line is that there is not one moment when we are left alone. God never leaves our side. Whatever the grief may be, whatever the trouble we bear, whatever the circumstance in which life places us, a compassionate God is present.

The president of a Christian university found himself on a flight where a little lady asked him to exchange seats with her so she could sit by a friend. He did and soon found himself engaged in conversation with a TWA pilot en route to his next flight. He realized that it was Captain John Testrake, who had been hijacked by terrorists in the Middle East. He and the people on his plane were threatened with death. The university president asked Captain Testrake, "What was the most life-changing development to come out of the entire incident for you?"

Without any hesitation Testrake said, "I knew the presence and the power of God unlike any other time in my life. I felt his presence in the cockpit. In fact, it seemed like there were two of me there. I could see myself standing and talking and making decisions and could feel another me across the cockpit. I knew that God was in that plane."

Testrake then related that during the hijacking, he had plenty of time to read the Bible in the cockpit and had discovered Deuteronomy 31:6, which encouraged him: "Be strong and courageous. Do not be afraid or terrified because of them, for the

LORD your God goes with you; he will never leave you nor forsake you."

When the hijacking ended, Testrake traveled to meet his wife in Germany. When they got to their room, his wife said, "John, I want to show you a Scripture verse I discovered that has sustained me all through the ordeal." She opened her Bible and turned to Deuteronomy 31:6. After they realized that they had each separately been hanging on to the same passage of Scripture thousands of miles apart, they began to question each other about the hour and the day they had been led to this verse. They had discovered the verse at about the same time.[3] Not for one moment will you be left alone.

III. *Comprehensiveness of Assurance*

Last, the reality of this amazing trust in Psalm 121 is reflected in the comprehensiveness of assurance in verses 7 and 8. These verses do not mean that Christians are removed from adversity, conflict, or distress. One pastor has said that for all people, in all walks of life, adversity is unexplainable, unavoidable, and unselective. The difference for the followers of Christ is the assurance, "He will watch over your life" (v. 7). Someone has said, "If the soul is kept, all is kept. God is the soul keeper of the soul."[4] He keeps our souls, as one has written, "in all circumstances and occupations of life, trips away from home and back, the kids on their way to school and on their way home, no matter what, day and night."[5] That watch is not only for the future but also for the here-and-now. The dimensions of his care are eternal, from the cradle to the grave and beyond. "We live with one foot in heaven and one hand in the firm, warm grasp of Eternal Love."[6]

If a backyard campout was interrupted by a storm, we always had a safe place. And in our fear we could run into our father's house. We go to the Father's house today with our sorrows and tears and there find blessed assurance for our troubled days. The words of the psalmist encourage us to remember:

Who? "The LORD."

What? "Will keep you."

When? "Your coming and going."

How long? "Forevermore."

What then? "I will lift up my eyes."

Chapter 20

All the Days of My Life
(General)

Psalm 23

The movie *The Elephant Man* is based loosely on the true story of John Merrick, a hideously deformed young man who lived in the 1880s during the time of England's industrial revolution. Known in the circus sideshows as "The Elephant Man," Merrick was thought to be an idiot incapable of feeling or speech. He lived a cruel, demeaning life until rescued by Sir Frederick Treves of the London Hospital.

Treves, a lecturer in anatomy at the Medical College, first saw Merrick as a "specimen" to analyze. However, his compassion for John grew daily. Treves sought to care for him, but hospital policy did not permit "incurables" to be admitted permanently because space was limited. The hospital administrator asked Treves to show him the deformed man so he could evaluate whether Merrick was capable of being helped. Central to the decision was whether the young man could think and speak as a normal person.

Treves began a crash course to prepare Merrick to meet the hospital administrator who would decide his fate. Among the sentences which Merrick practiced repeating after Treves were the first three verses of the Twenty-Third Psalm.

At two in the afternoon on the following day, the three met. The administrator asked simple questions. Although Merrick responded, his answers seemed to be by rote.

Carr Gomm, the administrator, had heard enough. He turned to leave and, as he and Treves paused in the hall after closing the door, they heard John Merrick begin to recite the Twenty-Third Psalm. This time, however, John did not merely echo Treves. He continued the psalm beyond what his mentor had taught him, saying ever more forcefully, "Yea, though I walk through the valley of the shadow of death, I will fear no evil: for thou art with me."

Treves realized he had not taught that part of the psalm to Merrick. He persuaded Carr Gomm to return to the room. They learned from John, who was now calm enough to speak, that his mother had taught him the psalm as a child. The crisis was solved, and John became to all who met him a model of what true humanity is.

The film *The Elephant Man* is an eloquent witness to the meaning of Psalm 23. This psalm is a cry to God in a time of great need. It is the poetic cry of a person shaken, one in the midst of danger, one in need of help. It is a psalm for us to sing when crisis threatens.[1]

When we lose a loved one to death and our hearts are broken, it is right to turn to God. This psalm is called by many "the pearl of the Psalms." More hymns are based on this psalm than any other. It is the most requested when sorrow, grief, anxiety, and uncertainty grip our hearts. Its focus is not on the psalmist, his troubles, or his enemies. The focus is on God and his character. It has been said that the psalm is so familiar it could breed contempt, because familiarity breeds contempt. However, on the contrary, it breeds contentment as we look to its words for hope and strength.

I. Foe

David begins by looking to the foe of his life: "The LORD is my shepherd." What do shepherds do? One of their tasks is to protect the sheep from predators, because sheep are the most helpless of all animals. We have a foe who is the enemy of our souls. His name is Satan. He desires to defeat and destroy us. God intervenes for us by being our Shepherd in the person of Jesus Christ. Jesus said, "I am the good shepherd." And what does the Good Shepherd do? He "lays down his life for the sheep" (John 10:11).

When faith is placed in Jesus Christ as our Savior to deliver us from sin and Satan, he becomes the Shepherd and Overseer of your souls (1 Pet. 5:2). He becomes our Savior first, then our Shepherd. It's a personal relationship. David did not say "a shepherd" or "the shepherd," but "my shepherd." Someone has said this psalm is the "I/He Psalm" as David uses *I, my,* and *me* seventeen times, as well as *he* and *his* thirteen times. We are comforted to know that we have Jesus as our shepherd friend to defeat our foe.

II. Fullness

Then, we see that the Shepherd is the fullness of our lives. In verses 1b–3, that is powerfully clear. An old saint put it this way; "The Lord is my shepherd, He's all I want." Notice how this fullness is demonstrated.

First, he is the fullness of rest: "He makes me lie down in green pastures." In the original language, *green pastures* means "green shoals in the midst of a dry, barren land." The Shepherd provides a rest for our spirit.

Second, he gives us the fullness of refreshment: "He leads me beside quiet waters," literally "waters of rest." Sheep prefer to drink from still waters rather than running water. In our sorrow, he will refresh our wounded hearts. "I will refresh the weary and satisfy the faint" (Jer. 31:25).

Third, he gives us the fullness of restoration: "He restores my soul." To restore means "to refresh, to return." When sheep fall on their backs they cannot get up by themselves. They are referred to as "cast sheep." If the shepherd does not get there within a reasonably short time, the sheep will die. The sheep become vulnerable to attack from wild animals as well as an illness that causes them to swell up, then circulation ceases, which brings on certain death. When the owner finds a cast sheep, he lifts it gently to its feet and rubs its legs to restore circulation until the sheep regains equilibrium and can walk steadily.[2]

We can be sure that our Good Shepherd will give whatever is needed to face these days of sorrow and readjustment. "No test or temptation that comes your way is beyond the course of what others have had to face. All you need to remember is that God will never let you down; he'll never let you be pushed past your limit; he'll always be there to help you come through it" (1 Cor. 10:13 The Message).

And finally, God guarantees the fullness of the right way: "He guides me in paths of righteousness for his name's sake." Sheep have no instinctive guidance system. They are easily lost. They need more guidance than any other livestock. You can be sure as you face tomorrow that your Shepherd will be there to guide you in every decision, at every crossroad, in every need. "I will instruct you and teach you in the way you should go; I will counsel you and watch over you" (Ps. 32:8).

III. Fears

This psalm next assures us that the Good Shepherd will escort us through the fears of life. Verse 4 says *even*. The King James Version uses the word *though*, but it may also be translated *when*. Everyone will walk through the valley of the shadow of death. That is a given. When we do, he dispenses two instruments to get us through: the staff, which keeps us safe because it is guiding us, and the rod, which is a short club that is heavy on one end and reinforced with nails, to defend us when we are attacked. The staff keeps us close and the rod keeps us safe. Both are symbols of intimacy, of the Good Shepherd walking with us through these frightening experiences.

Notice how the grammar shifts significantly at this point. David moves from speaking of God in the third person (he) to the second person (you). He has been speaking *about* God. Now in the valley, he turns and speaks *to* him. God becomes a reality when he becomes a necessity. The dark valleys make God more real to us than ever before.[3]

Ron Mehl has fought cancer for many years. Through his experience he has learned much about life and God, and he writes: "Shadows can cause us no harm; the shadow of a bear can't bite you, the shadow of a lion can't defeat you, the shadow of a giant can't intimidate you, the shadow of death can't conquer you."[4]

In the midst of this valley of shadows, the Shepherd does an amazing thing: He is expecting us. We're not unexpected drop-ins! He prepares a table for me in the midst of my enemies, a place of refuge. In the eastern culture, hospitality meant protection. He refreshes us by "anointing our heads with oil." The oil was used for soothing and healing. In aching, grieving hearts, you can be sure that in the days ahead, you will receive the oil of grace for your broken hearts.

IV. Future

Finally, God's provision is assured all the days of our lives, which includes all of the future of our lives: "Surely goodness and love will follow me all the days of my life" (v. 6). The heavenly escorts stand with us as God's sentinels day and night. Behind every tear, every grief, every broken heart, every long night of uncertainty, these security guards will flank your journey. They take us all the way to the Father's house. And then we will meet the Good Shepherd face-to-face. He, whom we have not seen except through the eyes of faith, we will see completely.

Kathy Sansovini was a healthy four-year-old when it was discovered that she had a rare muscular disease. The parents were driven to their knees, asking God to heal her. Finally they came to the place where they dedicated Kathy to the Lord and asked for his will to be done. One day, about a week before her death, she and her father were reading one of her favorite books. Suddenly, as if she forgot to tell him something important, Kathy said, "Daddy, do you know what? I'm going to heaven." Her daddy, somewhat startled, asked her why she said that and how she knew. Kathy replied, "Jesus came to me last night and told me he wanted me to come to be with him." She never again asked that God would heal her.[5]

"There remaineth therefore a rest to the people of God" (Heb. 4:9 KJV). What an amazing, marvelous hope we have in the Shepherd, who has prepared a place for us and assures us that we will rest with him forever. This Shepherd, Jesus Christ, promises, "He calls his own sheep by name and leads them out . . . he goes on ahead of them, and his sheep follow him because they know his voice" (John 10:3–4).

The LORD is my shepherd,
I shall not be in want.
> *All the days of my life.*

He makes me lie down in green pastures,
He leads me beside quiet waters.
> *All the days of my life.*

He restores my soul.
He guides me in paths of righteousness
For his name's sake.
> *All the days of my life.*

Even though I walk
Through the valley of the shadow of death,
I will fear no evil,
For you are with me.
> *All the days of my life.*

Your rod and your staff,
They comfort me.
> *All the days of my life.*

You prepare a table before me
In the presence of my enemies.
You anoint my head with oil;
My cup overflows.
> *All the days of my life.*

Surely goodness and love will follow me
All the days of my life,
And I will dwell in the house of the LORD
Forever.

All the days of my life.

Yes, we can be assured of God's provision . . . all the days of our lives!

Chapter 21

The Christian's Victory Over Death
(General)

John 11:25–26

The cape at the southern tip of Africa used to be called the Cape of Storms. Many vessels were beaten by the storms and disappeared forever in those treacherous waters. But then brave sailors began to steer sturdier ships through the storms to the quieter waters on the eastern side of Africa. And people began to think differently about the cape. They gave it a new name: the Cape of Good Hope. Because of Jesus Christ, we can talk about death as a passageway to hope . . . to a new and fuller life.

Phillips Brooks said, "We can live nobly now because we are to live forever."[1] Yet, as followers of Jesus Christ, we realize that death is an enemy. We grieve at the loss of our loved one. It has been well said that "the Christian hope for life beyond death is a hope that has passed through the furnace of suffering and death. Christians affirm the good news of Easter only in the wake of

Good Friday. Our hope for everlasting life permits no evasion of death's hard reality."[2]

The anguish of death invaded the home of Mary and Martha when their brother Lazarus died. He had been dead four days when Jesus arrived at their home. Jesus was met with the rather harsh statement—nearly an accusation—from Martha that if Jesus had been there Lazarus would not have died.

Jesus' response to her has brought assurance and hope to Christians for twenty centuries. While he was stating in bold terms who he was, his own victory over death, and victory for all those whose faith is in him, he was also answering the question from one of the great men of the Bible: Job. Job, who had suffered great loss and had seen death knock on the door of his family many times, asked, "Have the gates of death been opened unto thee?" (Job 38:17 KJV).

I. Age-Old Question

It is an age-old question. People for centuries from every corner of the world have grappled with it through philosophy, religion, and rituals. Man has sought for immortality. On the third floor of Southern Baptist Theological Seminary in Louisville, Kentucky, is a body of a deceased woman lying in a glass box. She is an Egyptian mummy named Sheret Mehyet; but everybody calls her "Sheri" for short. Sheri was the daughter of an Egyptian priest. She lived some twenty-seven hundred years ago during the days of King Hezekiah of Judah and Isaiah the prophet.

The Egyptians believed that the spirit could only inhabit a complete body after death. So embalming become a highly developed art. Sheri is a mute testimony to the skills of Egypt's ancient morticians. After almost three thousand years, her teeth, tongue, eyelids, and other body parts are still intact. But despite their cosmetic skill, those ancient embalmers were as powerless before death as we are. They could dress it up a bit, but they couldn't prevent it.[3]

II. Anguished Question

It is an anguished question. There is no escape from death. Its cold hand ultimately knocks at every door. Years ago, there was a magician in the United States by the name of Houdini. He was known as the great escape artist. One man said, "That man could escape from anything—except your memory." He conquered jails, trunks, chains, handcuffs, but after a lecture on a college campus, a student pounded him in the stomach, his appendix ruptured, peritonitis set in, and he died on October 31, 1926. Houdini's only failure was his failure to escape from death.[4]

III. Argued Question

It is an argued question. Books are written about it. Lectures are given about it. Debates are dedicated to it. Hoaxes and speculations abound about it. Man has been baffled, befuddled, bewitched, and bewildered about it. Only one authoritative answer has been given to Job's question and that of all humanity.

It is the words of the conqueror of death, our Lord Jesus Christ: "I am the resurrection and the life" (v. 25). Death, by his victory, became the victim! Death tried to swallow him, but he swallowed it and stood triumphantly over death, having killed death dead.

Reunion. Because of Christ's victory, what does this mean to the person who has trusted him as Savior and Lord? It means we will have a reunion with our loved ones who have gone before us and who will follow after us. In the Old Testament, the people of faith were said to be "gathered to his people." That did not mean they were put in the ground or in a tomb like everyone else. It meant the joining together of spirit in heaven.

Mangosuthu Buthelezi is a Christian and political leader in South Africa whose grandson was killed in an automobile accident. At the memorial service he said, "I feel an enormous loss which is indeed the loss of part of my own self. I feel a sudden lack of the oxygen I breathe and the food which nourished my soul and uplifted my spirit . . . even as I bow under the burden of this loss, I know that we are sustained by the hope of eternal life. Surely I shall see Nkosinatini again. We shall walk together again, and laugh and talk together. His body which has been broken in this life shall be made whole on the day of resurrection when I shall look again at my beautiful grandson and thank God for his mercy which endures forever."[5]

Repealed. For the Christian, it means the penalty of sin has been repealed. When our loved ones put their faith in Jesus Christ, the judgment of sin on all humans was revoked. "The

Spirit of life in Christ, like a strong wind, has magnificently cleared the air, freeing you from a fated lifetime of brutal tyranny at the hands of sin and death" (Rom. 8:1–2 The Message).

Rewards. For the Christian, it sets the stage for rewards. In eternity, there is judgment for those who have refused to accept Christ's love and forgiveness. In the Scriptures, this judgment sentences these individuals to hell. For the Christian there is judgment for the service we render in the name of Christ after conversion. The Bible mentions a series of crowns given to believers. They are God's rewards for faithfulness in service for his kingdom. "Well done, good and faithful servant" are the words every believer yearns to hear from Jesus on that day of rewards.

Rejoice. For the Christian, it means rejoicing, because we are in the presence of our Lord Jesus Christ. Paul said, "We . . . prefer to be away from the body and at home with the Lord" (2 Cor. 5:8). It is a homegoing for the believer. Going home is always exciting for us in this world. Going off to college, long trips, military service, or jobs that took us away—these gave us a sense of expectancy as we geared up to return to our loved ones.

John MacArthur states it well: "Simply put, we're going to be with a person as much as we are going to live in a place. The presence of Christ is what makes heaven, heaven."[6] "The Lamb is the light thereof" (Rev. 21:23 KJV).

Reminder. Then, the Christian's victory over death is a reminder to all of us to be "stedfast, unmoveable, always abounding in the work of the Lord" (1 Cor. 15:58 KJV).

- We are to be *firm* ("stedfast"), which means to be "firmly situated, settled in faith."
- We are to be *faithful*, "always abounding in the work of the Lord."
- We are to be *fruitful*. "Labour . . . not in vain in the Lord." Doing God's work means we don't come up empty. It is a time for us to redeem the time. A time to make life count. The psalmist said, "Teach us to number our days aright, that we may gain a heart of wisdom" (Ps. 90:12).

Death reminds us that we don't have all the time in the world. It helps us refocus on eternal values so we don't get our lives cluttered up with trivia. It tells us of the value of relationships.

Relationship. The Christian's victory over death is a call to everyone to be sure of a personal relationship to Jesus. It is as simple as the truth stated in Romans 10:9: "If you confess with your mouth, 'Jesus is Lord,' and believe in your heart that God raised him from the dead, you will be saved." Then, you can face the future, not as the French writer François Rabelais did nearing his death, when he said, "I am going to the great perhaps,"[7] but with confident assurance.

When Leighton and Jeanie Ford lost their son, Sandy, Leighton wrote a book entitled *Sandy, A Heart for God* in which he related one of the "conversations" he had with Sandy.

> During the months following Sandy's death, to cope with my grief and sense of loss, I kept a journal.

Through a series of "conversations" with Sandy, I continued to express my grief and bring our relationship to a close.

In one of those chats, I said, "Sandy, you've been dead two months earth time."

"I feel as if I have been alive forever, Dad. It's a lot like one big long today."

"It's a matter of time, Sandy, except that time heals. It's more a matter of nearness. I guess I'm concerned that as our time goes on, we will lose any sense of nearness."

"But why, Dad? You're moving closer to eternity every day. You're no longer moving from me, but to me! And besides, the 'Wall' between is so thin—you would laugh if you could see it."

"I think more of you than when you were at Chapel Hill."

"Sure! I know you do. I hear those thoughts."

"Night, Son! Enjoy the stars!"

"It's morning here, Dad. Enjoy the light!"[8]

Jesus' words of assurance ring clearly in the hearts of our faith. "I am the resurrection and the life. He who believes in me will live" (John 11:25).

In their song "Because He Lives," Bill and Gloria Gaither sum it up. Because Jesus has known victory over sin and the grave, we can confidently put our faith in God. We can have hope because he lives. Each day is brightened with confidence because our future is in his hands. Believers are resurrection people. We have victory over death because he lives!

Chapter 22

The Teacher Called Death
(General)

Hebrews 9:27

Teachers play an important part in the human experience. All people in one way or another, for better or worse, are affected by the teachers in their lives. Some of these mentors are parents. Some are in our school systems. Some are brothers and sisters. Some are classmates. Some are found in the church. Some are those encountered at the office. Some are lecturers or seminar gurus. They impact our lives from the cradle to the grave.

There is one teacher that we do not like to listen to. But this teacher raises our awareness about one of life's most important mysteries and realities. The teacher's calling card is marked *Death*. It is said that a mediocre teacher tells. The good teacher explains. The superior teacher demonstrates. The great teacher inspires.[1] The death of a loved one becomes a teachable moment. Let's listen while God's Word speaks to us about death. [*Read Heb. 9:27 at this point.*]

I. Reality

First, we are reminded of the reality of death. Our text speaks briefly but clearly. Everyone is going to die. More than one person is dying every second—4,000 an hour, 96,000 a day, more than 35,000,000 a year. Some people refuse to think about death. Some are nonchalant about it. Others live in fear of it. And some deal with it through the eyes of Christian faith. It comes down every highway, across every sky. Saint and sinner, rich and poor experience it. It is no respecter of persons.

II. Reason

The logical question is, Why does death exist? What is the reason for death? The Scriptures tell us that death entered the planet of earth when the first man and woman rebelled in disobedience to God's clear command. He had instructed Adam and Eve, "You must not eat from the tree of the knowledge of good and evil, for when you eat of it you will surely die" (Gen. 2:17).

Man did what God forbade. Death—an intruder, an alien to God's desire for mankind's good—came. Since Adam represented the human race, all humanity inherited his tragic death genes. It may not seem fair, but it's like a football team being penalized for the error of one player. One man costs the whole team. God must keep his Word.

III. Realm

When you consider death, you must look at the realm of death. The separation of the soul from the body is far more than physical. It is also spiritual—the alienation of the spirit from God—and it is eternal. Physical death awaits every human. Spiritual and eternal death are for all who are outside the grace and forgiveness of Jesus Christ, "for the wages of sin is death" (Rom. 6:23). It is a terrible payday, but a very real one.

IV. Readiness

Facing these realities, it is crucial for every person to make the proper plans for this journey. The more significant the journey, the more thorough our preparations. There must be a readiness for death. The psalmist underscored it when he wrote, "Teach us to number our days aright, that we may gain a heart of wisdom" (Ps. 90:12).

How can we do it? First, we can think about death honestly. Contemplate the reality that we will not always be in this world. Parents should help their children to develop a philosophy of life and death. This can be done in progressive steps as they mature. Adults should have some things settled about death. For example, have you made your will? If you don't, the state will do it for you. And your hard-earned assets could be dispersed away from those people, the church and philanthropic ministries you love most. What about your place of burial, as well as the type and setting for your memorial service?

Second, death teaches us to make time count. "There is a time for everything, and a season for every activity under heaven" (Eccles. 3:1). Someone wrote it this way: "So valuable is time that God gives only a moment of it at once, and he gives that moment but once in eternity."[2]

Third, death teaches us about eternal values. What is important in life? Some years ago a college football team won a hard-fought bowl game. The fans and team were ecstatic over the big victory. During the celebration in the locker room, word came that the head coach's father, a spectator at the game, was fatally stricken with a heart attack. Suddenly, the atmosphere changed. Tears, silence, and sadness filled the room that only moments before had been alive with happiness. A player speaking to the press remarked that victory in the football game seemed insignificant in the light of the death of the coach's father.

Fourth, death instructs us about the significance of relationships. Never take for granted a spouse, a child, a grandchild, a cherished friend or colleague, a parent or grandparent. People are at the heart of who we are. Cherish every shared experience, the memories of special occasions. Make new memories. Write notes of love and gratitude. Give something you value to someone you value.

Don't be afraid to say *I love you*. A bereaved husband, in reflecting on the sudden death of his wife, said that the thing hardest for him to deal with was remembering hearing her say *I love you* and kissing him as he went off to work.

Keep short accounts with disagreements and anger. Be quick to say *I'm sorry* and *Forgive me*. Mend broken fences. Seek to live in your relationships so that regret will not be your companion in years ahead.

Fifth, death underscores the most important preparation of all, preparing to go into eternity to face God. The Old Testament writer Amos said it in one terse sentence: "Prepare to meet your God" (Amos 4:12).

Our New Testament text repeats it: "After this [death] the judgment" (Heb. 9:27 KJV). There is only one way to be prepared for death. And that is to place faith in the only one who conquered death: Jesus Christ. "The wages of sin is death, but [and here is the great, good news] the gift of God is eternal life through Christ Jesus our Lord" (Rom. 6:23).

There is no better time than right now to settle your eternal destiny and to receive Jesus Christ as your personal Savior and Lord. It is simple. "Everyone who calls on the name of the Lord will be saved" (Rom. 10:13).

In a line that never seems to end, a remnant of faithful communists stand in respectful silence in the winter winds at Red Square in Moscow waiting to enter the mausoleum of Nikolai Vladimir Lenin, the revered patriarch of Russian communism. They have come to view a dead body. But there is no thought that Lenin lives and is not there.

In the center of a public cemetery in Springfield, Illinois, rises an obelisk. It sits atop an appropriately modest private mausoleum. On the wall surrounding the monument are the seals of the states of the Union. Under the floor is buried all that is mortal of President Abraham Lincoln. Visitors read the famous statement of Edwin Stanton, "Now he belongs to the ages." They come to pay homage to the man who preserved the Union. But there is no thought that Lincoln lives and is not there.

In Paris, France, a giant sarcophagus sits under the gilded dome of Les Invalides, a military hospital. Within that tomb rests the mortal remains of Napoleon Bonaparte. Tourists gaze in awe at the gigantic tomb of the great emperor. But there is no thought that Napoleon lives and is not there.

But when pilgrims go to the tomb of the Lord Jesus Christ outside the walls of Jerusalem, they are visiting a place that is no longer occupied. The very meaning and message of this tomb is its emptiness. Our Lord is not there. He is risen![3]

V. *Results*

Death teaches us the final results of life's choices. For all whose faith is in Jesus Christ, one nanosecond after death they will be in the presence of Jesus Christ. "Today you will be with me in paradise" (Luke 23:43) was his promise to the dying thief. It is the same Savior who gives the same promise to all who have trusted him.

For those who refuse, the choice is a disastrous one. John writes in Revelation 20:11–12, 15: "Then I saw a great white throne and him who was seated on it. Earth and sky fled from his presence, and there was no place for them. And I saw the dead, great and small, standing before the throne, and books were opened. Another book was opened, which is the book of life . . . If anyone's name was not found written in the book of life, he was thrown into the lake of fire." Tough words, but words not to be taken lightly. No one should live an undecided life. Choose life today. Learn the lessons from death, apply them to your own spiritual condition, and live now and forever in Jesus Christ, who conquered death.

Richard DeHaan, a marvelous Bible teacher and radio preacher, had two sons: Richard and Marvin. One day they were playing in an orchard near several bee hives. They irritated the bees and one made straight for Richard's head and zapped him. The other boy began to cry and scream as the bee darted for him. DeHaan explained that the bee had only one stinger and Richard, unfortunately, had received it. The bee could buzz Marvin but it could not sting him. It had lost its power to sting.

Paul wrote, "Where, O death, is your sting? . . . Thanks be to God! He gives us the victory through our Lord Jesus Christ" (1 Cor. 15:55, 57). The judgment of God does not fall on those whose trust is in the Lord, who takes the sting of eternal death. Lessons about death, when properly applied to our lives, are invaluable for now and forever.

Chapter 23

What Jesus Did to Death
(General)

2 Timothy 1:8–10

Warren Buffet, the financial investment genius and one of the richest men in America, has his doubts about life beyond the grave. And this worries him. Buffet admits, "There is one thing I'm scared of. I am afraid to die." His biographer Roger Lowenstein writes: "Warren's exploits were always based on numbers, which he trusted above all else. In contrast, he did not subscribe to his family's religion. Even at a young age, he was too mathematical, and too logical to make the leap of faith. He adopted his father's ethical underpinnings, but not his beliefs in an unseen divinity." We are told that Buffet is stricken with one terrifying fear—the fear of dying.[1]

Death does something to us, but death also does something for us as Christians. A funeral or memorial service is better than a baptism or a marriage. Someone has said that funerals "press the noses of the faithful against the windows of their faith—the afterlife begins to make the most sense after life—when someone we love is dead on the premises."[2]

This isn't true for everyone. Karl Marx, father of communism, said that faith made people ignore the problems of the material world. Sigmund Freud said that Christianity was a wish-fulfillment religion. Jessie Ventura, former governor of Minnesota, said that religion was for wimps.

Someone has said that the Christian message of hope is not a belief that grew up within the church. It is the belief around which the church itself grew up and the given upon which its faith was based.[3]

Another person put it this way: "If the resurrection is not good news, there is no good news." Paul, near the end of his life journey, pointed this out in his letter to his protégé, Pastor Timothy. He said that Jesus "destroyed" or abolished death. The word *destroyed* means "to make thoroughly inactive." He whose earthly life began in the womb did not end in the tomb.

I. Incomprehensibleness

By abolishing death, he took out some of the incomprehensibleness of death. There is a certain mystery about death (1 Cor. 15:51). All other experiences—good and bad—have been witnessed to. But in death, no one has returned to talk about it, except Jesus Christ. Because he did, some of its mystery has been uncovered. Paul reported that in the "mystery" of death, we don't stay that way. We change. "Listen, I tell you a mystery: We will not all sleep, but we will all be changed" (1 Cor. 15:51).

Remember when your children were small and they would go to sleep in the car, on the floor, or in your arms? Then you would take them to their room, change them into their pajamas, and they would wake up the next morning, the same person but in different clothes! So it is for the Christian. They will awake in heaven the same person, but changed into a new and better body equipped for eternity.

II. Inevitability

Second, Jesus took away the inevitability of death—its seeming finality. In 1922 archeologist Howard Carter, who had been searching for the tomb of the Egyptian King Tutankhamen, finally unearthed it. He said he was struck dumb with amazement. "It was the most incredible cache of ancient treasure that anyone could remember." But with this discovery came good news and bad news. The good news was that the treasure and the wonderfully preserved mummy were still in the tomb. The modern world was able to behold the splendor of ancient Egypt! The bad news was that the treasure and the wonderfully preserved mummy were still in the tomb.

All those riches had been originally deposited in that tomb to accompany the pharaoh on his journey through the underworld. But the booty had not budged—and neither had the body! It was staggering proof that all the hopes of the ancient Egyptians were in vain.[4] That religion—and others like it—are dead and offer no hope for the gripping embrace of death. But Jesus does!

Death is a destroyer, but Jesus Christ is the great rearranger. Life starts out with the union of two invisible cells. They multiply. And in nine miraculous months, a human body is formed. Once outside the womb, that body continues to change and rearrange itself from baby to child, to youth, to adulthood, to senior adult, to death, to decay. Dust to dust. But Jesus came to "destroy death." Death becomes not the beginning of the end, but the end of the beginning.

Listen to the words of 2 Corinthians 5:1: "Now we know that if the earthly tent we live in is destroyed, we have a building from God, an eternal house in heaven, not built by human hands." That means at least three things:

1. Our "building," our body, is the one we now possess.

2. Our new building will be better than the one we have now.

3. It will be a body that is going to be like Jesus.

Scripture promises, "But we know that when he appears, we shall be like him, for we shall see him as he is" (1 John 3:2).

ALCOR Life Extension Foundation is located in Phoenix, Arizona. It promises to freeze the bodies of deceased individuals in liquid nitrogen. The hope they sell is the preservation of the body until science makes discoveries that can resurrect the dead. People can be frozen in time—for a fee, of course!

The great baseball slugger Ted Williams wrote a note shortly before his death, which stated his desire to be frozen after death: "JHW, Claudia, and dad all agree to be put into bio-stasis after we die. This is what we want, to be together in the future, even if it is only a chance."[5]

The reality of being together is not, for God's children, a chance but a certainty. The casket and grave become our hope chest.

III. Impact

Finally, Jesus destroys the impact of death, its power. Hebrews 2:14 states: "That by dying [Jesus] might crush him who wields the power of death" (Moffatt).

Why does death wield such power? Why does mankind look away from its cobra stare? Because it carries with it the sense of the unknown, of separation from family, friends, and familiar surroundings. Apart from Christ, there is the frightening reality of eternal separation from God and eternal punishment. But Jesus Christ "crushed" the one who had previously had death at his command. The word the writer of Hebrews uses here is powerful. To *crush* or *destroy* means to "render inoperative." It's like the removal of the battery from a car. It renders the car inoperative. So, too, with death for the believer. Jesus, by his resurrection and by guaranteeing our own, has taken the battery out of death.

Three-year-old Jordan Lee was at choir practice with her parents before the coming Easter celebration. Jordan Lee knew about Jesus' dying on the cross and his dying for our sins. Referring to the choir's anthem, her father asked her, "What does it mean, 'after three days?'"

The preschooler replied, "It means he rose from the dead."

"What does that mean? What does Easter mean?"

Her response was perfect: "We didn't have to be scared any more."[6]

Because Jesus overcame death, we live in expectant hope. This world is not our home. Death makes us absent from the body, but it also ushers us into the presence of the Lord. Paul stated it this way: "For to me, to live is Christ and to die is gain" (Phil. 1:21). To live as Christ is to conquer death as he did. What Jesus did to death enables us to do the same thing. "We are more than conquerors through him who loved us" (Rom. 8:37).

Chapter 24

First Steps

(Service for Mothers of Aborted Children)

Acts 27:14–29

[This service is very important as it becomes a part of the healing process for the mothers. It is a part of dealing with grief that they live with daily. It is a time for release and closure. It is a time for remembering as well as anticipating. The following are suggested procedures, a sample program, and a message outline to assist caregivers and pastors in a commemorative ceremony that will honor Christ and restore spiritual and emotional health.]

Suggested Procedures

1. Before the service, have the women who have lost (or aborted) unborn children to pick a name that they would have given their children.

2. Encourage these women to write a poem or eulogy about their children.

3. Have a pianist playing background music or play recorded music of hymns and praises.

4. Have a candelabra at the front of the room with a candle for each baby represented.

5. Give a program to all who participate in the service with the names of the children who are being memorialized. [*See sample program on page 176–80.*]

6. Pastor, compassionate church members, family members, and caregivers should be present early to greet and hug each woman as she arrives.

7. A small chapel or room is probably best for the occasion.

8. Have a red rose individually wrapped with fern or baby's breath in a basket visible during the service to be presented at the end of the service to each woman for each child being presented.

9. On a pedestal in the front of the room have a floral basket with the names of each baby on a card placed in the arrangement. The women take the names with them after the service.

10. If the women have prepared their eulogies or poems, give time for them to be read. When finished, each woman can light the candle representing her child.

11. Read Scriptures such as Psalm 23; Psalm 25:1–7; Psalm 46:1–5; Psalm 86:1–7; Psalm 103:1–7; Psalm 121:1–2; Psalm 139:13–17; Isaiah 49:15; Jeremiah 1:5; Revelation 21:1–4.

12. Bring a brief message. [*See message on page 180–84.*]

13. Pray for the women, asking God's grace, peace, and renewal.

14. Have the women return to their candles, pray silently as they release their babies by name into the hands of Jesus, asking in return for God's complete healing of their memories and emotions as they extinguish their candles.[1]

15. Immediate family members or special friends can be invited, but these should be limited in number.

Sample Program

First Steps
Memorial Service

1. Front cover: a picture of a baby's hand in the hand of an adult or another symbolic picture or sketch.

2. Under the front cover picture: Have the words from Psalm 139:13–14: "For you created my inmost being; you knit me together in my mother's womb. I praise you because I am fearfully and wonderfully made."

3. Inside left page: Print the following poem.

PRECIOUS

I took from you the chance to run, to laugh, to grow, to play.
But know for sure, the love I send you, this special day.
The world may look upon your life as not deserving birth;
But I know deep within my soul, you have a priceless worth.

I wonder if your eyes are blue or green or brown or gray.
But this I know . . . and it's for sure . . . you are in God's care
to stay.
My precious one: someday we'll meet, when I pass Heaven's
gate.
And then, we'll sit and hug and share. Oh! I can hardly
wait.
Though I look to the day to come; I'll reunite with you.
For now, I'll rest in Jesus' grace, for He's cleansed and made
me new.[2]

4. Under the poem: Have "With Tribute and Love to . . . " and list the chosen names for the unborn children.

5. Inside right page: Have a small picture of flowers or trees at the top of the program. Under that put the date and the name of the pastor or friend who is bringing the message of hope. Then print the following words:

Behold! We now enter his gates with thanksgiving and his
courts with praise.
Behold! Old things are now passed away and *all* things have
become new!
Behold! The Lamb of God, Who takes away the sin of the
world!
Behold! The Lord God of heaven hath become our salvation
and our song.
Behold! The King of glory, the Bright and Morning Star, the
gentle Shepherd, the Alpha and Omega, the Wonderful

Counselor, the covenant-keeping God, the Great Physician, the Holy One of Israel, our Lord and Savior. Amen.

[*This can be read aloud as a group or as a responsive reading.*]

6. Back cover: This page can be filled with Scriptures or perhaps a meaningful poem or eulogy presented at a previous memorial service or from another appropriate source. It can also be used to give more information on the names of the babies being memorialized. Examples:

Hannah

Literal meaning: "Grace"

Suggested Scripture: Psalm 84:11

"For the LORD God is a sun and shield; the LORD bestows favor and honor; no good thing does he withhold from those whose walk is blameless."

Daniel

Literal meaning: "God is my Judge"

Suggested Scripture: Psalm 7:10

"My shield is God Most High, who saves the upright in heart."

7. The following prayer is one that can be placed in the program or made available as a book or Bible marker:

LISTEN TO JESUS AS HE SPEAKS TO YOU

My little one,
I know your heart.

Do not be afraid.
I understand all
that is in your life.

My heart broke
as you were broken.
Know that I am
with you still.

I will never abandon you.
Nor will I ever reject you.
I will always love you.
That is my promise
to you.

I will help you keep chaste
in body, mind, and spirit.
Live close to my heart.
And seek out my plan
for your life.

I love you more
than anyone
could ever
dream
of loving you.

> My dear friend,
> My precious friend,
> I love you.³

> > I will not forget you!
> > See, I have engraved you
> >   on the palms of my hands
> >   —Isaiah 49:15–16

Message Outline

Anchors That Hold in the Storm
Acts 27:14–29

A pastor interviewed a seasoned Christian counselor and talked to her about grieving. He asked her what she advises people to do when they're dealing with losses. She said, "Of course, I tell them to feel their feelings. But then I also urge people to reduce radically the pace of their lives. I urge them to review their loss, talk about it openly, think about it thoroughly, write about it reflectively, and pray through it. It's my experience that people want to run from their pain. They want to replace pain with another feeling as soon as they can. To recover from pain, you have to face it! You must stand in it and process it before it will dissipate. That's God's way."⁴

This service is dedicated with that purpose in mind. These words are directed to bring hope in the midst of sorrow. Our text comes from an experience in the life of the apostle Paul. He was a prisoner of Imperial Rome aboard a ship taking him to trial. While en route, their ship ran into a terrible storm, what is known as a northeaster. The men tried desperately to save themselves and the ship. Paul had a word from God. He was promised safe passage for himself and every passenger. Since the ship was being driven toward some rocks that would rip it to pieces, the captain "dropped four anchors from the stern and prayed for daylight" (v. 29). If I were to name each anchor that held them steady in the storm, I would give them the following names. These names represent the comprehensive nature of God's goodness in the storms of our lives.

I. Anchor of His Presence

The first anchor is the anchor of his presence. From God's first walk with Adam in the Garden of Eden to his traveling with the nation of Israel in the form of a pillar of fire and a cloud of smoke, to his being with the judges, prophets, disciples, and followers, God is always reaching out to assure us of the fact of his presence. He has given us today, in the absence of his physical presence, his Holy Spirit: "I will ask the Father, and he will give you another Counselor to be with you forever—the Spirit of truth . . . I will not leave you as orphans; I will come to you" (John 14:16–18).

At the Nazi prison camp at Auschwitz, a group of Jewish people, including an eight-year-old boy, were being lined up for the gas chamber. The little boy was very much afraid and began to cry. An orderly standing nearby had a candy bar in his pocket. Knowing how long it had been since the boy had seen candy, the orderly pulled it out, unwrapped it, and handed it to the boy. Still crying, he took a bite and gave it back. The line was getting shorter and the boy was becoming more terrified. Suddenly, the orderly did an amazing thing. He said to the boy, "Dying isn't so hard. Let us do this together." And he took the boy by the hand and walked in.[5]

II. Anchor of His Power

Second, we have the anchor of God's power. The angel messenger said to Paul, "Do not be afraid" (v. 24). Courage draws from the springs of God-given power. To face our fears, our pain, and our dark valleys, we are able to navigate them through his power. "In Him who strengthens me, I am able for anything" (Phil. 4:13 Moffatt).

Some people will tell you to pull yourself up by your bootstraps and you'll get over it. One woman who had suffered a huge loss in her life responded to those well-intended words, "Some days I can't find my bootstraps. In fact, some days I can't even find my boots."[6] Don't wish your will away or try to will it away. Face it. Feel it. Grieve. His power will enable you to keep on keeping on.

III. Anchor of His Purpose

Then, there is the anchor of his purpose. Paul knew, as unpleasant as the prospect, he "must stand trial before Caesar"

(v. 24). God, in his sovereign providence, would use this date with destiny for something good. God doesn't waste our sorrows. When life tumbles in on us—sometimes by our choices, sometimes by circumstances—we are not to be overwhelmed. God is bigger than our sins, our situations, our sorrows. One of the greatest verses in the Bible is given to affirm us in that certainty: "And we know that in all things God works for the good of those who love him, who have been called according to his purpose" (Rom. 8:28).

IV. Anchor of His Peace

Finally, we have the anchor of his peace. "I have faith in God" (v. 25). The angel promised safety, Paul believed it, and that settled it. Just as surely as the dawn broke over the anchored ship in the stormy sea, the sunrise of hope will shine more brightly for you in the days ahead. God will open the eyes of your heart to his peace. You will find yourself amazed when that peace comes to you. It may come when you least expect it. It may come when you need it most. It may come in the night. It may come when you're down; it may come when you're up. But it will come. And you will know it is the one who promised, "Peace I leave with you; my peace I give you. I do not give to you as the world gives. Do not let your hearts be troubled and do not be afraid" (John 14:27).

About 150 years ago, Luther Bridgers, a recent seminary graduate, was spending a weekend with his parents, his wife, and their five children. That night the house caught fire and burned to the ground. Bridgers and his parents escaped, but his wife and five children died in the flames. In his desperation and depression, he cried out to God, "O God, give me a song. Somehow give me a song to know that you are there." And God did. Bridgers wrote down the following lyrics:

There's within my heart a melody.
Jesus whispers sweet and low,
"Fear not I am with thee, peace be still
In all of life's ebb and flow."
Jesus, Jesus, Jesus, sweetest name I know.
Fills my every longing, keeps me singing as I go.

The world doesn't understand it, but those who know God and his peace do. He is real. He is there. He is here. He's not asleep at the switch. He loves us.[7] Those anchors will hold until the dawn breaks.

Notes

Chapter 1

1. Mack Waters, *The Encyclopedia of Christian Quotations* (Grand Rapids: Baker Books, 2000), 111.

Chapter 2

1. Joseph Bayly, *The View from a Hearse* (Elgin, Ill.: David C. Cook Publishing, 1973), 65.
2. Billy Graham, *Facing Death* (Minneapolis: Grason, 1987), 79.
3. Marshall Shelley, "Two Minutes to Eternity," *Christianity Today* (1994), 25.
4. Quoted in Paul Powell, *Death from the Other Side* (Dallas: Annuity Board of the SBC, 1991), 27.
5. From a letter sent by Paul Kuck to friends. Author of poem is Walter Ketcham, Orlando, Florida, December 2001. Used by permission.
6. Erwin Lutzer, *One Minute After Death* (Chicago: Moody Press, 1997), 76.

Chapter 3

1. Author unknown, *Orlando Sentinel*, 2001.
2. Lloyd Ogilvie, *Ask Him Anything* (Waco: Word Books, 1981), 46.
3. Adrian Rogers, *God's Way to Health, Wealth, and Wisdom* (Nashville: Broadman Press, 1987), 56–57.
4. Richard Halverson, "Perspective," a bi-weekly devotional letter, McLean, Virginia, January 25, 1989.
5. Steve Farrar, *Anchor Man* (Nashville: Thomas Nelson, 1998), 170.
6. Charles Schultz, "Peanuts," *Winston-Salem Journal*, February 23, 1962, as quoted in Jack Ricks Noffsinger, *It's Your Turn Now* (Nashville: Broadman Press, 1964), 41.
7. Permission to include this charge to the other students granted by Brent's mother, Tracy Bolin.
8. R. Kent Hughes, *Romans* (Wheaton: Crossway Books, 1991), 170–71.

Chapter 4

1. John Hewitt, church newsletter, First Baptist Church, Asheville, North Carolina, date unknown.
2. E. C. McKenzie, *14,000 Quips and Quotes* (Grand Rapids: Baker Book House, 1980), 374.
3. Charley Reese, "Samurai Wisdom: We are all alike in that one day we will die," *Orlando Sentinel* (July 25, 1999).

4. George Morrison, *Morrison on Mark* (Ridgefield: AMG Publishers, 1997), 100.

5. Author unknown.

6. R. Kent Hughes, *Mark* (Westchester, Ill.: Crossway Books, 1989), 2:148.

7. Eulogy by Richard Downes, given at memorial service for his wife, Beverly, June 3, 2003, Orlando, Florida.

8. Malcolm Muggeridge, *Confessions of a Twentieth Century Pilgrim*, as quoted in church bulletin, Branch's Baptist Church, Richmond, Virginia, November 21, 1999.

Chapter 5

1. Robert J. Morgan, *Nelson's Complete Book of Stories, Illustrations, and Quotes* (Nashville: Thomas Nelson, 2000), 191.

2. Ibid., 185.

3. Scott A. Wenig, "Hide and Seek," *Preaching*, January-February, 2001, 27.

4. Les Parrott II, *Rev.*, July-August 2002, 33.

5. Bob Buford, *Half Time* (Grand Rapids: Zondervan, 1994), 32.

6. Josiah Gilbert Holland (1819–1881), quoted in Steve Farrar, *Finishing Strong* (Sisters, Oreg.: Multnomah, 1995), 75.

7. Stu Weber, *Tender Warrior* (Sisters, Oreg.: Multnomah, 1993, 1999), 206.

8. Erwin W. Lutzer, *Your Eternal Reward* (Chicago: Moody Press, 1998), 160.

Chapter 6

1. John Maxwell, "Which Chair Do You Sit In?" *Discovery*, June 1996, 2.
2. Karen Howe quote, *Eternity*, December 1974, 11.
3. Timothy K. Jones, "The Daddy Track," *Christianity Today*, June 16, 1989, 16.
4. Personal letter from Fay Dallas to author, April 12, 1989. Used by permission.
5. John Huffman, *Preaching*, May-June 1990, 27.
6. Walter Wangerin Jr., "Gentle into That Good Night," *Christianity Today*, November 6, 1987, 25.

Chapter 8

1. Helmut Thielick, source unknown.
2. Mary A. Baker, *Peace Be Still* (1941).

Chapter 9

1. William E. Brown, *Bryan College Newsletter*, 2001, 1.
2. James Dobson, *When God Doesn't Make Sense* (Wheaton: Tyndale House Publishers, 1993), 83–89.
3. Cited in ibid., 27–28.
4. Alvera Mickelson, "Why Did God Let It Happen?" *Christianity Today*, March 16, 1984, 23.

5. Cited by Philip Yancey, "Surprised by Shadowlands," *Christianity Today*, April 4, 1994, 112.

6. Cited by Gary C. Redding, "Are You Afraid of the Future?" *Preaching*, January-February 1998, 32.

7. Vance Havner, "Why?" *Fundamentalist Journal*, May 1986, 19.

8. Dale Ralph Davis, *Such a Great Salvation* (Grand Rapids: Baker House, 1990), 95.

Chapter 10

1. James Clemons, *Sermons on Suicide* (Louisville: Westminster/John Knox Press, 1989), 87.

2. Paul Scherer, "God's Claim on a Man's Mind," in *Twenty Centuries of Great Preaching*, edited by Clyde E. Fant Jr. and William M. Pinson Jr. (Waco: Word Books, 1971), 10:331.

3. Clemons, *Sermons on Suicide*, 44.

4. Billy Friel, *What Should I Do When* (Nashville: Broadman Press, 1990), 18.

5. Clemons, *Sermons on Suicide*, 81.

6. Ibid., 142.

7. Ibid., 19.

8. Paul Powell, *Death from the Other Side* (Dallas: Annuity Board of the SBC, 1991), 46.

9. Vernon Grounds, *Ministry*, September 1999, 11.

Chapter 11

1. Personal letter to author from Kenyan pastor Julius Wafula Macheusi, June 10, 1998.
2. Cited by Erwin Lutzer, *Growing Through Conflict* (Wheaton: Victor Books, 1992), 82.
3. Craig Wahlund, Hope Presbyterian Church, Minnesota (date unknown).
4. Robert Ozment, *When Sorrow Comes* (Waco: Word Books, 1992), 19–20.
5. Ibid., 47.
6. Cited in Brian Harbour, *Living Joyfully* (Nashville: Broadman Press, 1991), 39.
7. Harry Rimmer, "Our Last Trip Will Be a Round Trip," *Pulpit Helps*, April 1997, 17.

Chapter 12

1. Author unknown, *USA Today*, July 12, 1995, n.p.
2. John Wesley White, *Preaching*, January-February 1988, 28.
3. Ibid., 30.
4. Erwin Lutzer, *Growing Through Conflict* (Victor Books, 1992), 103.
5. William Barclay, *And Jesus Said* (Philadelphia: Westminster Press, 1970), 164.
6. Ron Lee Davis, *The Healing Choice* (Waco: Word Books, 1986), 121.

7. Steve Brown, "New Year New Land," *Key Life*, January-February 1991, 3.

8. Ike Reighard, "SBC Pastor's Conference, June 1993," *Proclaim*, fall 2002.

Chapter 13

1. Buddy Scott, *Relief for Hurting Parents* (Nashville: Thomas Nelson, 1989), 93–94.

2. Robert J. Morgan, *Nelson's Complete Book of Stories, Illustrations, and Quotes* (Nashville: Thomas Nelson Publishers, 2000), 450–51.

3. Source unknown.

4. Greg Laurie, *The God of the Second Chance* (Dallas: Word Publishing, 1997), 183–84.

Chapter 14

1. Author unknown.

Chapter 15

1. Russell Bradley Jones, *Gold From Golgotha* (Chicago: Moody Press, 1945), 29.

2. Steven J. Lawson, *Heaven Help Us* (Colorado Springs: Navpress, 1995), 120–21.

3. Ibid., 190.

4. Erwin Lutzer, *One Minute After You Die* (Chicago: Moody Press, 1997), 78.

5. Spiros Zodhiates, *Life After Death* (Ridgefield: AMG Publishers, 1997), 101.

6. Max Lucado, "From Jericho to Jerusalem," *Preaching Today,* March–April 1993, 12.

Chapter 16

1. J. Michael Shannon, "To Illustrate," *Preaching* September-October 2001.

Chapter 17

1. J. I. Packer, *Knowing God* (Downers Grove: InterVarsity Press, 1973), 147.

2. Kyle Yates, *Preaching from Great Bible Chapters* (Nashville: Broadman Press, 1957), 36.

3. Ken Taylor, *My Life: A Guided Tour* (Wheaton: Tyndale House Publishers, 1991), 9.

4. Elizabeth George, *The Lord Is My Shepherd* (Eugene, Oreg.: Harvest House Publishers, 2000), 177–78.

5. Cited in David Roper, *Psalms 23: The Song of a Passionate Heart* (Grand Rapids: Discovery House Publishers, 1994), 158.

6. Mitch Albom, *Tuesdays with Morrie* (New York: Doubleday, 1997), 173–74.

7. Phillip Keller, *A Shepherd Looks at Psalm 23* (Grand Rapids: Zondervan, 1970), 173–74.

8. Anne Graham Lotz, *Heaven: My Father's House* (Nashville: W Publishing Group, 2001), 18–19.

9. Mark Lowry, E-mail to author, October 18, 1999.

Chapter 18

1. W. A. Criswell and Paige Patterson, *Heaven* (Wheaton: Tyndale House Publishers, 1991), 7.

2. Joseph Stowell, *Eternity* (Chicago: Moody Press, 1995), 81–82.

3. *Orlando Sentinel*, February 6, 1993, E–8.

4. Erwin Lutzer, *One Minute After You Die* (Chicago: Moody Press, 1997), 65.

5. Cited in D. P. Brooks, *Dealing with Death, A Christian Perspective* (Nashville: Broadman Press, 1974), 114.

6. James Dobson, "The Most Valuable Legacy," *Home Life*, June 1995, 33.

Chapter 19

1. Lloyd Ogilvie, *Falling into Greatness* (Nashville: Thomas Nelson, 1984), 192.

2. Ibid., 194.

3. Jim Sells, newsletter, chancellor of Southwest Baptist University, Bolivar, Missouri.

4. Graham Scroggie, *The Psalms* (Old Tappan, N.J.: Fleming H. Revell Co., 1978), 208.

5. Walter Kaiser Jr., *The Journey Isn't Over* (Grand Rapids: Baker Book House, 1993), 38–39.

6. Ron Mehl, *The Night Shift* (Sisters, Oreg.: Multnomah, 1994), 112–13.

Chapter 20

1. Robert K. Johnston, *Psalms for God's People* (Ventura, Calif.: Regal Books, 1982, abridged), 73–75.
2. Phillip Keller, *A Shepherd Looks at Psalm 23* (Grand Rapids: Zondervan, 1970), 60–63.
3. David Roper, *Psalm 23: The Song of a Passionate Heart* (Grand Rapids: Discovery House Publishers, 1994), 108–10.
4. Ron Mehl, *Surprise Endings* (Sisters, Oreg.: Multnomah, 1993), 163.
5. Mr. and Mrs. Edward Sansovini, from their testimony tract, Boca Raton, Florida, 1960.

Chapter 21

1. Cited in Willard Scofield, *Decision*, April 1982, 7.
2. Denyse O'Leary, "Tissues of Lies," *Christianity Today*, October 23, 2000, 118.
3. Robert B. Setzer sermon illustration, *Proclaim*, October 1982, 26.
4. Moody Adams, newsletter, date unknown, 3.
5. Personal correspondence to author from Cliff Gosney, Daytona Beach, February 7, 2001.
6. John MacArthur, *The Glory of Heaven* (Wheaton: Crossway, 1996), 142.
7. Sermon illustrations, *Proclaim*, date unknown, 32.
8. Leighton Ford, Sandy: A Heart for God (Downers Grover, Ill.: InterVarsity Press, 1985), 171, as quoted in

Stephen Brown, *When Your Rope Breaks* (Nashville: Thomas Nelson, 1988), 183.

Chapter 22

1. E. C. McKenzie, *14,000 Quips and Quotes* (Peabody, Mass.: Hendrickson Publishers, 1980), 501.

2. John Wanamaker, quoted in Eleanor Doan, *The New Speaker's Sourcebook* (Grand Rapids: Zondervan, 1968), 356.

3. Jimmy Draper, "The Empty Tomb," www.LifeWay.com, April 9, 2001.

Chapter 23

1. Cited in *Dynamic Preaching,* December, 2001, 38.

2. Thomas Lynch, "The Undertaking: Life Studies from the Dismal Trade," *Christianity Today,* October 23, 2000.

3. C. S. Dodd as quote by Landrum Leavell III in "The Reafile," newletter of Royal Palms Baptist Church, April 12, 1995.

4. Timothy Floyd, "Life After Death," *Proclaim,* spring 2001.

5. Author unknown, *Orlando Sentinel,* July 26, 2002.

6. Author unknown, "First Baptist Reporter," Amarillo, Texas, April 13, 2001.

Chapter 24

1. Ken Freeman, *Healing the Hurts of Abortion,* Women's Manual, 89.

2. Lynn Kennedy, member of First Baptist Church, Orlando, Florida, missionary to Burkina Faso. Used by permission.

3. Angelo J. Damiano, *No More Shall I Mourn*, pamphlet, Linking Education and Medicine, 1990.

4. Bill Hybels, "A Better Kind of Grieving," *Preaching Today*, tape #108.

5. Letter from a client to Christian counselor Dwight Bain, August 26, 1996.

6. Ike Reighard, *Treasures from the Dark*, workbook (Quantum Leap Productions, 1998), 6.

7. Al Meredith, Wedgwood Baptist Church, message reported in Baptist Press, September 19, 1999.